MALACHI

J. Vernon McGee

THOMAS NELSON
Since 1798

NASHVILLE   DALLAS   MEXICO CITY   RIO DE JANEIRO

Published in Nashville, Tennessee, by Thomas Nelson, Inc.

Scripture quotations are from the KING JAMES VERSION of the Bible.

Library of Congress Cataloging-in-Publication Data

McGee, J. Vernon (John Vernon), 1904–1988
   [Thru the Bible with J. Vernon McGee]
   Thru the Bible commentary series / J. Vernon McGee.
     p.   cm.
   Reprint. Originally published: Thru the Bible with J. Vernon McGee. 1975.
   Includes bibliographical references.
   ISBN 0-7852-1036-9 (TR)
   ISBN 0-7852-1095-4 (NRM)
   1. Bible—Commentaries. I. Title.
BS491.2.M37 1991
220.7′7—dc20   90–41340
ISBN: 978-0-7852-0623-1   CIP

Printed in the United States

16 17 QG 14 13

CONTENTS

MALACHI

PREFACE

The radio broadcasts of the Thru the Bible Radio five-year program were transcribed, edited, and published first in single-volume paperbacks to accommodate the radio audience.

There has been a minimal amount of further editing for this publication. Therefore, these messages are not the word-for-word recording of the taped messages which went out over the air. The changes were necessary to accommodate a reading audience rather than a listening audience.

These are popular messages, prepared originally for a radio audience. They should not be considered a commentary on the entire Bible in any sense of that term. These messages are devoid of any attempt to present a theological or technical commentary on the Bible. Behind these messages is a great deal of research and study in order to interpret the Bible from a popular rather than from a scholarly (and too-often boring) viewpoint.

We have definitely and deliberately attempted "to put the cookies on the bottom shelf so that the kiddies could get them."

The fact that these messages have been translated into many languages for radio broadcasting and have been received with enthusiasm reveals the need for a simple teaching of the whole Bible for the masses of the world.

I am indebted to many people and to many sources for bringing this volume into existence. I should express my especial thanks to my secretary, Gertrude Cutler, who supervised the editorial work; to Dr. Elliott R. Cole, my associate, who handled all the detailed work with the publishers; and finally, to my wife Ruth for tenaciously encouraging me from the beginning to put my notes and messages into printed form.

Solomon wrote, ". . . of making many books there is no end; and much study is a weariness of the flesh" (Eccl. 12:12). On a sea of books that flood the marketplace, we launch this series of THRU THE BIBLE with the hope that it might draw many to the one Book, The Bible.

J. VERNON McGEE

MALACHI

Malachi

The Book of
MALACHI

INTRODUCTION

Malachi brings down the curtain on the Old Testament. He is the last in a long succession of prophets who foretold the coming of the Messiah. In fact, if we were to go back one thousand years before Malachi and then come down through the centuries, we would find that God was increasing the tempo of telling the people about the coming of the Messiah. And the last voice is that of this man Malachi. I like to think of him as a sort of radio announcer for the Lord. It is as if he were saying, "The next voice you hear will be John the Baptist four hundred years from now." Well, four hundred years is a long time to wait for station identification!

Malachi is a very interesting person although we know nearly nothing about him. We will find that he has a wonderful sense of humor. I do not think you can be a prophet or a preacher without a sense of humor, and if you haven't found humor in the Bible, my friend, you are not reading it aright.

We will also see that this man Malachi in a very definite way was a messenger. The name *Malachi* means "my messenger." The Septuagint gives its meaning as "angel," since *angelos* is the Greek word for "messenger." An angel was a messenger and could be either human or supernatural. In fact, there were a few church fathers who actually thought that Malachi was a *spiritual* angel, that an angel wrote this book—but there are no grounds for this. At the opposite extreme we have the liberal school of higher criticism which claims that the book is actually anonymous. They argue that Malachi means just messenger, that it is only a title and not a name at all. Our information of

Malachi is as limited as it is regarding angels. If the book were anonymous, it would be the only book of prophecy to be so, and I do not think that Malachi would want to be the exception to the rule, especially since he was the last one to write.

There is a reason that we do not know very much about Malachi. He is a messenger, God's messenger with a message, and frankly, we don't need to know about the messenger. When the Western Union boy rings your doorbell at one o'clock in the morning with a very important message for you, you do not question him about his ancestors! He doesn't tell you all about himself and his family. You're not interested in the Western Union boy's ancestors, and you don't care whether or not they came over on *The Mayflower*—especially at one in the morning! The fact of the matter is that you don't even get his name. The important thing is *the message* that he brings. Malachi was just a messenger, and the important thing is the content of his message.

We have this same method used by the Spirit of God in the Gospel of Mark where the Lord Jesus' genealogy is not given at all. The reason is that each of the four Gospels presents Christ in a different way. Matthew presents Him as the King. If He's the King, He will have to be in the line of David, and that is the way the Gospel of Matthew opens: "The book of the generation of Jesus Christ, the son of David . . ." (Matt. 1:1). The important thing is that He is the Son of David because Matthew is presenting Him as the King. But when you come to the Gospel of Mark, which presents Him as the Servant of God, Mark is not concerned about giving His genealogy, and there's none given. The important thing about a servant is whether or not he can get the job done. That is the thing you want to know about anyone who comes into the place of service for you. And Mark shows that the Lord Jesus could get the job done, and He *did* get it done. In the same way, it is *the message*, not the messenger, which is important in the prophecy of Malachi.

There is some difference of opinion about the time at which Malachi wrote. The date that I suggest is 397 B.C., which is probably a late date. It is the belief of conservative scholars today that Malachi prophesied in the last part of the fifth century. That would be near 397 B.C.

but somewhat earlier than that. The important thing is that Malachi was the prophet at the time of Nehemiah as Haggai and Zechariah were the prophets at the time of Zerubbabel and Joshua. This man Malachi concluded the prophetic books as Nehemiah concluded the historical books of the Old Testament. He probably prophesied during the time of Nehemiah's governorship or immediately afterwards.

As we have said, Malachi was a messenger, but the thing that is important is his message. He himself uses the term *messenger* three times, and he makes three tremendous and significant references to other messengers.

1. In Malachi 2:7 he refers to Levi as the messenger of the Lord: "For the priest's lips should keep knowledge, and they should seek the law at his mouth: for he is the messenger of the LORD of hosts." This suggests that every messenger, every witness, every teacher of the Word is an angel of the Lord, a messenger of the Lord. In the Book of Revelation where we have the messages addressed to the seven churches, it is expressed in this way: "Unto *the angel* of the church of Ephesus write . . ." (Rev. 2:1, italics mine). I believe that this means the messenger of the church—not a supernatural being, but just the human messenger—in other words, the pastor of the church. I was a pastor for a long time, and I rather like this idea of calling the pastor an angel. I've heard him called everything else, so I don't know why we shouldn't include "angel."

2. Malachi also announced the coming of John the Baptist as "my messenger." "Behold, I will send my messenger, and he shall prepare the way before me . . ." (Mal. 3:1). John the Baptist was the Malachi of the New Testament and began where the Malachi of the Old Testament left off.

3. The third reference to a messenger is to Christ as "the messenger of the covenant." Again in Malachi 3:1 we read, ". . . and the LORD, whom ye seek, shall suddenly come to his temple, even the messenger of the covenant, whom ye delight in: behold, he shall come, saith the LORD of hosts." The angel of the Lord in the Old Testament is definitely the preincarnate Christ.

I want you to see something that makes Malachi one of my favorite books of the Bible (of course, I have sixty-five other favorite books in the Bible), and that is that Malachi has such a wonderful sense of humor. He had to have one in order to deal with the group he had to deal with in that day. He adopted a question-and-answer method. First, he would quote a declaration or an interrogation which God had made to Israel. Then he would give Israel's answer which in every case was supercilious and sophisticated sarcasm. It was arrogant and haughty and presumptuous and even insulting. But, believe me, Malachi has some good answers from the Lord! And since they are the Lord's answers, it is the Lord who has a sense of humor. I hope you enjoy this book because it is a great little book, by the way.

OUTLINE

OUTLINE

CHAPTER 1

THEME: *The love of God for Israel; the priests reproved for profanity*

Malachi is going to deal with those same problems with which Nehemiah dealt, and this reveals that Malachi was speaking into that day. The first problem is the defilement of the priesthood. The second is their foreign marriages and the divorce of their Israelite wives—believe me, God is going to come down hard on this. Many folk ask me to deal with the subject of divorce. Well, I take whatever comes up in the Word of God, and God will talk about divorce in Malachi. Then the third problem is that the people of Israel were neglecting their giving of the tithe and the offering to God. You can be sure that you won't like what God has to say about those who are kidding everybody about their giving to the Lord.

The burden of the word of the LORD to Israel by Malachi [Mal. 1:1].

Malachi means "my messenger." He is the Western Union boy who brings the last message from God to the people of Israel.

"The burden of the word of the LORD to Israel." A "burden" is a judgment, a judgment from God, and it will be a very strong and rigorous rebuke that God will give to them.

Something else that we should note is that Malachi is addressing Israel, that is, all of the twelve tribes. It is obvious that the tribes of Israel didn't really get lost. Although they seem to be "lost" to some people today, they never were lost. This message is "to Israel," to all twelve of the tribes. There had returned to the land just a remnant from each tribe, very few from each one. But God addressed them, and very frankly, I think that Malachi's message went out from here to the others who had not returned. The Book of Nehemiah reveals that there was communication back and forth. There were messengers, travelers, going back and forth between Israel and the place of captivity where they had been in slavery. We are going to see that, apparently, the message went out to all twelve of the tribes.

> **I have loved you, saith the LORD. Yet ye say, Wherein has thou loved us? Was not Esau Jacob's brother? saith the LORD: yet I loved Jacob,**
>
> **And I hated Esau, and laid his mountains and his heritage waste for the dragons of the wilderness [Mal. 1:2–3].**

Malachi's message starts out in this very marvelous, wonderful way: "I have loved you, saith the LORD." Isn't that a wonderful way to begin!

Now how do you think that these people are going to respond to that? Remember that they have returned to the land, and by the time of Nehemiah, although they are discouraged about the rebuilding of the walls of Jerusalem, there is a show of prosperity, and they are going through the form of worship in the rebuilt temple. They are going through the ritual of it, and on the surface everything looks good. But, oh, are they a sarcastic, supercilious, sophisticated, blasé group! God says to them, "I have loved you, saith the LORD," and listen to them!— "Yet ye say, Wherein hast thou loved us?" Can you believe that these people would have the audacity to speak to God like that? I'm not sure but what there are a great many people today in the church who would raise that same question and say, "Look at the things that are happening to us today. How can you say that God loves us?" Well, God made it very clear to Israel from the very beginning that He loved them.

It is interesting that you go a long way into the Bible before you find God telling anybody that He loved them. But when you get to Deuteronomy (by that time you've come to Moses), you're out in the wilderness and you've been out there for forty years, and it is going to be pretty hard to make anybody believe that God loves him. But listen to what Moses says in Deuteronomy 10:15: "Only the LORD had a delight in thy fathers to love them. . . ." God simply had not been saying that to anyone. You go through the time of the Flood and afterwards, and God never told anybody that. God didn't tell Abraham that He loved him, but He did, of course. The point is that God was in no hurry to let mankind know that He loved them. But He says here, "Only the LORD had a delight in thy fathers to love them, and he chose their seed after them, even you above all people, as it is this day."

Now God is prepared to prove what He has said, and His answer is this: "Was not Esau Jacob's brother? saith the LORD: yet I loved Jacob, and I hated Esau, and laid his mountains and his heritage waste for the dragons of the wilderness." This is a tremendous statement that God makes to them. The people were questioning, they were doubting the love of God, and God reminds them of the origin of their nation. Jacob and Esau were twins. God made a difference between them at the very beginning (see Gen. 25:22–23), but it was about fifteen hundred years before He stated as He does here that He loved Jacob.

This presents a problem: Why should God say that He loved Jacob and hated Esau? A student came to the late Dr. Griffith Thomas with that question. "I have a problem," he said. "Why does God say that he hated Esau?"

"Well, I have a problem with that verse, too," Dr. Thomas replied. "But my problem is why God said that He loved Jacob. That's the real problem."

My friend, the real problem here is why God would say that He loved this people. But let's understand one thing: God never said this until Jacob and Esau had become two great nations which had long histories. Therefore, God said that He loved Jacob because of the fact that He knew what was in Jacob's heart. He knew that here was a man who had a desire for Him and that Esau did not have a desire for Him at all. But it had to be worked out in fifteen hundred years of history before God was prepared to make the kind of statement He makes here in Malachi. We need to understand that the difference here between loving and hating is simply that the life of the nation that came from Esau, which is Edom, and the life of the nation which came from Jacob, which is Israel, demonstrate that God was right when He said that He loved one and hated the other.

All this reveals something that we need to face up to today. We have majored so much on the love of God. Do you know that if God loves, God also hates—because you cannot love without hating? As someone has said, love and hate are very close together. If God loves the good, He has to hate the evil—it couldn't be otherwise—and that is exactly what we find here. The histories of the nation of Israel and the nation of Edom are altogether different. God says that because of Esau's life, because of the evil which was inherent in this man and which worked itself into the nation of Edom, He is justified in making this statement.

> Whereas Edom saith, We are impoverished, but we will return and build the desolate places; thus saith the Lord of hosts, They shall build, but I will throw down; and they shall call them, The border of wickedness, and, The people against whom the Lord hath indignation for ever.
>
> And your eyes shall see, and ye shall say, The Lord will be magnified from the border of Israel [Mal. 1:4–5].

What God is saying to them is this: "My action and conduct with these nations which came from Esau and Jacob reveal that I loved Jacob and that I hated Esau." After God judged Edom, they never made a comeback. When was the last time you saw an Edomite? They are just not doing business today. They went out of style years ago. God judged Edom, and this action of His looks like loving and hating. And God says to Israel, "I demonstrated that I loved you." At the beginning, He never made that statement because He had to wait until it worked itself out. This reveals, therefore, that God's choice is neither capricious nor arbitrary. God does not make choices like that. There has to be something to back it up. God had a real relationship with His people. He was the Father of the nation; He was their Lord, their God, and also their Judge. And he judged them most severely. In fact, it would seem that later on He judged Israel more severely than He judged Edom—but that was when Israel rejected the Messiah.

There is a great deal said today about "God is love." It is an abstract statement to say that God is love. He says, "I have loved you and I have demonstrated it." God was a long time telling the human family that He loved them, but He demonstrated it long before He said it. He demonstrated it from the very beginning—in the lives of Adam and Eve, from the time of the call of Abraham, and right down to the present.

A son honoureth his father, and a servant his master: if then I be a father, where is mine honor? and if I be a master, where is my fear? saith the LORD of hosts unto you, O priests, that despise my name. And ye say, Wherein have we despised thy name? [Mal. 1:6].

"A son honoureth his father, and a servant his master: if then I be a father, where is mine honor?" Now God was never Father to an *individual* Israelite. Even of both Moses and David, the best that was said was that they were servants of Jehovah—each was a servant of Jehovah. But God called the whole nation His son. He reminds them that He has this relationship with the nation.

"And if I be a master [that is, your Lord], where is my fear? saith the LORD of hosts unto you, O priests, that despise my name. And ye say, Wherein have we despised thy name?" They are greatly offended that God would say this about them. They say, "My, we're such nice, wonderful little Sunday school boys and girls. We go to the temple, we go through the rituals, we are very faithful, and we are really the pillars of the whole nation of Israel. And then You dare ask us about despising Your name? How in the world are we despising Your name?"

Of course, you've got to go way back into "uncivilized" times to find children honoring their parents. The modern way and the civilized way is not to honor your parents. But back in that day they did, and so God uses that as the illustration: "A son will honor his father, and a servant his master, but you don't honor Me." This is something that should have gotten to them, but it didn't get to them because they had a hard shell about them. They were a very arrogant and haughty and self-sufficient people. You couldn't tell them anything. I am of the opinion that that is a picture not only of youth today but of all people. We accuse young people of not listening, but the older folk are not listening either—they certainly are not listening to God at all. God said to Israel, "You despise My name." And they act hurt; they act as if they really don't know what He is talking about. Very frankly, had you been in Jerusalem in that day, you would have seen the crowds flocking into the temple. They were bringing their sacrifices. They were going through the ritual. They gave an outward show of being very religious. Their pious performance was very impressive. I am sure that most of us would have said, "This certainly is an alive group, and they're certainly worshiping God." To tell the truth, they were very far from God. Down underneath they actually despised His name.

> **Ye offer polluted bread upon mine alter; and ye say, Wherein have we polluted thee? In that ye say, The table of the LORD is contemptible [Mal. 1:7].**

How can they despise His name when they were going to the temple so regularly? God begins to lay it out for them: "Ye offer polluted bread upon mine altar." I think we should make it very clear that the bread refers to the offering that was made on the altar. It would be what we would call a meat offering, that is, it would be an animal sacrifice. God will make it clear in verse 8 that that is really what He is talking about.

God says that their sacrifice was polluted, but they wouldn't acknowledge that. They ask the question, "Wherein have we polluted thee?" My, are they offended that God would dare say this to them because they are such lovely people! To pollute God, by the way, was a serious charge if it were true, but the people dismiss the charge with an indifferent nod of the head and a pretended ignorance. They act as if God doesn't know what He is talking about.

Then God says to them, "In that ye say, The table of the LORD is contemptible." They said that it was contemptible, and they despised it by the way they treated it and by the way they acted.

God is speaking to these people, the Jewish remnant which has returned to the land and has settled upon their lees. They are very happily situated now. They have been back for over one hundred years. The Captivity is now in the background, and things are prosperous in the land. They've become just a little self-sufficient. They have a temple now, and they are going through the ritual of it, but they actually are far from God. They have become insolent as they talk back to God as He says things to them. Maybe you will want to tune me out because what the Lord says now is really going to hurt.

And if ye offer the blind for sacrifice, is it not evil? and if ye offer the lame and sick, is it not evil? offer it now unto thy governor; will he be pleased with thee, or accept thy person? saith the Lord of hosts [Mal. 1:8].

"And if ye offer the blind for sacrifice, is it not evil? and if ye offer the lame and sick, is it not evil?" It is clear now that He is talking about *animal* sacrifices. God made it clear to Israel at the very beginning that nothing which was in any way maimed or defiled or any of that sort of thing was to be offered to Him. In other words, when you give secondhand clothing to the rescue mission, don't put that down on your books, thinking you will get credit from God. Don't misunderstand me—the mission can use the secondhand clothes, but you're not giving sacrificially to God when you give that sort of thing. Listen to the instructions God had given to them: "But whatsoever hath a blemish, that shall ye not offer: for it shall not be acceptable for you. And whosoever offereth a sacrifice of peace offerings unto the Lord to accomplish his vow, or a freewill offering in beeves or sheep, it shall be perfect to be accepted; there shall be no blemish therein. Blind, or broken, or maimed, or having a wen, or scurvy, or scabbed, ye shall not offer these unto the Lord, nor make offering by fire of them upon the altar unto the Lord. Either a bullock or a lamb that hath any thing superfluous or lacking in his parts, that mayest thou offer for a freewill offering; but for a vow it shall not be accepted" (Lev. 22:20–23).

God was telling them that the offering they offered was really a picture of the Lord Jesus Christ who is the perfect Lamb of God who takes away the sin of the world. Any imperfect offering was an insult to the Lord Jesus Christ. In case they missed it in Leviticus, God interprets the law for them in Deuteronomy 15:21: "And if there be any blemish therein, as if it be lame, or blind, or have any ill blemish, thou shalt not sacrifice it unto the LORD thy God."

Now what was happening in Malachi's day was something like this: Imagine there is a man living up in the hill country of Ephraim who has prize cattle. He always gets the blue ribbon at the cattle show. But one day his prize bull becomes sick, and when he calls the veterinarian, the veterinarian says, "I don't think he's going to make it. I think he'll die." So the man says, "Well, let's load him in the truck in a hurry and rush him down to the temple where I'll offer him for a sacrifice." When the man brings the bull to the temple, the priests can see that the old bull is sick, but they go through with it because this is a very prominent fellow who lives up in Ephraim, you see. But when the people see this prize blue-ribbon bull being offered, they say, "Mr. So-and-So sure is a generous fellow. Look at what he is offering to the Lord!"

What do we do today that corresponds to that which was taking place in Israel in Malachi's day? Remember that the apostle Paul described the men in the last days as "having a form of godliness, but denying the power thereof . . ." (2 Tim. 3:5). Men will be very pious. There is a great deal of pompous piousity that is demonstrated by many so-called Christians today. Paul describes them as "having a form of godliness." You can pour oleomargarine into a butter mold, and it may look like butter, it may even smell like butter, but it is not butter. You probably have heard the story of the very stingy man who gave his wife a mink coat—at least, it was supposed to be a mink coat. No one could understand why this man would be so generous until one day when he and his wife went walking down the street. As they passed a rabbit hound, the coat jumped off his wife and started running! It just happened to be rabbit, you see—not mink.

We should recognize God's rebuke here as a danger signal and as a red light for us. This is a message for folk who go to church—they listen, they are very orthodox, very fundamental, and they say amen. They know the language. They can quote any number of pious platitudes. They are satisfied with a tasteless morality. They go through a form of truth and all the shibboleths, and they are satisfied. But may I say to you, they actually *despise God* when they approach worship like that. It was Dr. G. Campbell Morgan who years ago made the statement, "I am more afraid of the profanity of the sanctuary than I am of the profanity of the street." The profanity of the streets is bad enough, my friend.

You may protest, "But I've never brought a sick cow to God and offered Him that!" Will you notice what God says here in our verse: "Offer it now unto thy governor; will he be pleased with thee, or accept thy person? saith the LORD of hosts." In other words, try paying your taxes with that old sick cow! This is a good question: Do you pay more in taxes than you give to the Lord? I want to say very candidly, shame on you if you are paying more taxes than you are giving to the Lord. I believe that when the offering is taken in the average church, there is actually lots more profanity taking place there than down in the slums of the city where the drunkards are. Why? Because there is a great deal of put-on, of hypocrisy, taking place in the sanctuary today.

I know a very prominent businessman who lives in the east. He's a man that I greatly respect, but I have suspected his generosity for many years. He likes to give, and he'll give generously if you'll put up a building with his name on it. When we obtained our new headquarters facilities some years ago, I had a suggestion or two from folk who would be glad to give if the building were named in their honor. We simply don't do business that way at the "Thru the Bible" radio ministry. When you give to this ministry, you're giving to get out the Word of God. You're not giving to get your name engraved on anything. I realize that our policy causes many prominent, wealthy people to turn from us, but that is perfectly all right. The Lord is speaking to a whole lot of other folk, and I rejoice in that. I happen to know that this particular businessman has buildings named for him on two college campuses. He's a big shot. When he gives, you can be sure it will be with the blowing of the horn, the blare of the trumpet, and the beating of the drum. The Lord Jesus told about the Pharisee who went down to the street corner to give to the poor, and he had somebody down there blowing a horn. Everybody said, "Oh, look at Pharisee So-and-So! Isn't he generous? He's down there on the corner, just giving money away to the poor!" One time this prominent businessman invited me out for an evening meal, and we had good fellowship. He's a likable fellow. He has real charisma. Afterwards, he came with me to the church where I was preaching that night. The pastor of the church invited him up to the platform to lead in prayer. He's a wealthy man, let me tell you, and so he was invited up there to lead in prayer. I saw with my own eyes that this man who had given the waitress a two-dollar tip for our dinner put only a one-dollar bill in the offering plate. I thought, *My, he didn't even tip God generously tonight!*

When the One who was here nineteen hundred years ago sat by the treasury and watched how the people gave, I am sure that some of them thought, "What business has He to see how I give?" He happened to be the Lord Jesus Christ, and I'm not sure but that on Sunday morning He looks over your shoulder as you give. Are you giving what you give for a good meal when you eat out? Are you giving as generously to the Lord's work as you do to other things where it makes a show? My friend, the old sick cow is still being taken to church today. That is the method that Israel used; and, believe me, the Lord didn't let it pass.

This is burning sarcasm—listen to Him: "And if ye offer the blind for sacrifice, is it not evil? and if ye offer the lame and sick, is it not evil? offer it now unto thy governor; will he be pleased with thee, or accept thy person? saith the LORD of hosts." I will say again, and it is none of my business, but I'm just telling you what the Lord says. He is saying here in a very definite way that you cannot bring Him a sick cow. You don't pay your taxes with a sick cow. Are you giving to the Lord as much or more than you are giving in taxes today? You may argue, "I *have* to pay my taxes." Yes, you sure do, but what about your giving to the Lord? That is supposed to be on the basis of love. The Lord Jesus said. "If ye love me, keep my commandments" (John 14:15). I do not think we are under the tithe today at all. It is interesting to note, however, that in the Mosaic Law there was more than one tithe; we know that there were two tithes, and many think that there were three tithes. That would mean that the people actually gave thirty percent of what they made to the Lord.

When the Lord Jesus looked over the treasury, He saw how the rich gave—and they gave large sums—but He didn't commend them for it because they kept so much more for themselves. But He saw the poor widow and those few coppers which she dropped in there—compared to the wealth of the temple, very candidly, she gave *nothing!* But the Lord Jesus took those copper coins, He kissed them into the gold of heaven, and He said that she gave more than anybody else.

I am amazed at how our Bible-teaching radio ministry is carried on. It is carried on by many widows who send a dollar bill, and they always say, "It isn't anything." Maybe in comparison to our costs, it isn't much, but when a whole lot of widows get together it sure makes an impression. It is the people who regularly send in the five-dollar and ten-dollar gifts that sustain this radio ministry.

The Israelites in Malachi's day were being very clever. When an old cow got sick or a lamb broke his leg, they would patch it up and rush it off to the temple to offer it as a sacrifice to God. God says that He will not accept such a sacrifice. I wonder how many offerings are really made acceptable to God today? We are told that any offering we make to God is like the priest making an offering back in Old Testament times. Believers today are priests before God, and we are to give by grace, but grace does not mean that we give as little as we possibly can. I am afraid that we are actually seeing a sacrilege committed in the church every Sunday. Someone will say, "But a sacrilege means that somebody steals something in the church." Yes, that is the meaning. The Israelites were guilty of sacrilege because their offerings really cost them nothing. They were valueless, though they may have been large. And, my friend, it is sacrilege to enter the church and put something into the offering plate when there is no blood or sacrifice on the gift.

Frankly, I think that it is sometimes wrong to give. Many people pay ten dollars to see a football or baseball game, and God says to them, "If you pay that kind of money for that and then come into My house and drop a one-dollar bill into the offering and think you have done something for Me, you are wrong. Why, you didn't even give Me the kind of tip that you give to a waitress!" This is pretty strong language here, is it not?

> **And now, I pray you, beseech God that he will be gracious unto us: this hath been by your means: will he regard your persons? saith the LORD of hosts [Mal. 1:9].**

Is it possible that these people could continue giving an outward show but not realize that in their hearts they are not right with God? Their hearts are polluted, and their offering, therefore, is polluted.

> **Who is there even among you that would shut the doors for nought? Neither do ye kindle fire on mine altar for nought. I have no pleasure in you, saith the LORD of hosts, neither will I accept an offering at your hand [Mal. 1:10].**

God says, "All this ritual that you are going through is meaningless. It is for nothing. It doesn't profit." But they continue on in it.

> **For from the rising of the sun even unto the going down of the same my name shall be great among the Gentiles; and in every place incense shall be offered unto my name, and a pure offering: for my name shall be great among the heathen, saith the LORD of hosts [Mal. 1:11].**

Israel was bringing the name of God into disrepute by the way they were serving Him. They were not serving Him as they did in the days of Solomon, for instance, when the Queen of Sheba was greatly impressed with what she saw. At this time, the unsaved were not impressed because it was just a form and a ceremony.

God says that there is a day coming when His name will be great among the Gentiles. If you think that this has been fulfilled today, you're entirely wrong. It will be fulfilled in the Millennium but not today. God's name is not great among the nations today.

"And in every place incense shall be offered unto my name, and a pure offering." "Incense" speaks of prayer. That "pure offering" is Christ.

"For my name shall be great among the heathen, saith the Lord of hosts." God's purpose in choosing Israel was that they might witness to the nations of the world.

> **But ye have profaned it, in that ye say, The table of the Lord is polluted; and the fruit thereof, even his meat, is contemptible [Mal. 1:12].**

The Gentiles profaned the name of God because of the lives and actions of God's people whose hearts were polluted and whose ritual was contemptible.

> **Ye said also, Behold, what a weariness is it! and ye have snuffed at it, saith the Lord of hosts; and ye brought that which was torn, and the lame, and the sick; thus ye brought an offering: should I accept this of your hand? saith the Lord [Mal. 1:13].**

"Ye said also, Behold, what a weariness is it! and ye have snuffed at it, saith the Lord of hosts." In effect they were saying, "It makes us tired to go to church, to go through all of these things. Oh, what a weariness!" My friend, when the heart is not in the thing, it becomes weariness.

One morning my daughter and I were driving in the morning rush-hour traffic. At the time I was a pastor in downtown Los Angeles. I couldn't wait to get to the church that morning. I had broadcast tapes to make, and I was looking forward to it. I said to her, "Look at the faces of all these people in this big traffic jam. They are bored to tears, dreading to go to work. The worst thing in the world that I can think of is to be doing a job you hate to do. It makes the hours long, and there is no joy in it whatsoever. Going to church is just as boring to a great many people." This is the reason we so often hear it asked, "What can we do to interest our people in the church?" Have you ever heard that discussed? Or, "What can we do to get people to come on Sunday nights?"Someone will suggest, "Let's serve a dinner. Let's have a banquet. Or let's have a little different service. Instead of all this boring Bible study, let's have some special music, and let's put on an entertaining program. We could have some sort of pageant."

What is wrong, my friend, when people are saying that God is becoming boring to them? Why do you think that men ever adopted a ritual to begin with? Why do they wear robes and chant and burn incense and march around? They are tired of spiritual worship—that's it—and they need something to tickle the flesh. Somebody says, "But I love an orderly service." I do too, but there is danger in loving order, and there is danger in loving a ritual.

I recognize that ritual has its place and that there are many fine folk who were brought up that way. When I was a pastor in downtown Los Angeles, I knew a lovely couple who really loved the Word of God but who were members of a very formal, a very high church. He was actually enraged by the informality of the way in which I began the service. He and his wife would not come until we had completed the brief preliminaries of the service. He very frankly told me, "I just can't stand that informality"—but he loved the Word of God, and so I forgave him the other.

Way back in the stern days of our fathers, the Puritans, they would sit on log benches and listen to a sermon for two hours. Today there are people who will sit on bleachers for three hours out in the hot sun to watch a baseball game. There are folk who will sit out in the cold to watch a football game. And there are those who will sit for three hours listening to an opera, or for two hours watching a movie, or for four hours to see *Hamlet*. I find it thrilling to sit and listen to a Shakespearean play. When my wife and I were at Stratford-on-Avon and saw *Richard III*, I didn't sit on the edge of my seat, but I sat back, relaxed, and thoroughly enjoyed it for three hours. My friend, why are you weary when your preacher speaks for one hour? I'm a long-winded preacher and always have been. I would speak for an hour, and do you know who complained about it? It wasn't the average person; many people said they didn't think it was too long. It was some of the leaders, the so-called spiritual leaders of the church, who complained. We love the ritual, and we love the form. We go to church, we stand up and sit down, and we sing the doxology loudly, but really where are our hearts? Do we do it because of a love for Him? Do we desire to worship Him? We sing, "Were the whole realm of nature mine, that were a present far too small." Is that a gift far too small? It sure is. Then why did you put just a dollar in the offering plate? If the whole realm of nature isn't big enough for a gift to God, then what about the dollar bill which isn't worth very much today?

It is so easy to get tired and weary in church work. Dwight L. Moody came home one time, and although he was very weary, he was going to another meeting without taking time out to rest. His family begged him to cancel it because he was so weary, but he said this, "I get tired in the work, but I never get tired of the work."

But cursed be the deceiver, which hath in his flock a male, and voweth, and sacrificeth unto the Lord a corrupt thing: for I am a great King, saith the Lord of hosts, and my name is dreadful among the heathen [Mal. 1:14].

"For I am a great King, saith the Lord of hosts, and my name is dreadful [to be reverenced] among the heathen." His name is going to be reverenced someday, but it's not reverenced even today.

One of the things that has brought God's name into disrepute has been the ministry and those who represent Him here, the believers. I don't question their salvation—and yet I'm afraid I do question the salvation of some. Have you ever noticed that God never called a real believer a hypocrite? But the Lord Jesus really laid it on the line when He was talking about the religious Pharisees of His day. Very frankly, He said terrible things about them. He called them "whited sepulchres." Can you imagine that? That was an awful thing to call these people, but that is what He called them. And He likened them to a dish that on the outside is beautiful, but on the inside it hasn't even been washed. It didn't get into the dishwasher, and it is filled with all kinds of garbage. The Lord Jesus said, "That's the hypocrite" (see Matt. 23:25–29). And that's what these people were in Malachi's day—they were merely going through a form of religion.

Let's put it on the line today: Do you have religion, or do you have

Christ? Are you real, or are you just going through the form of it? Do you wear your Christianity like a garment that you can take off and put aside at any time, and do you generally put it aside when you are not in church? Perhaps you assume a certain pious attitude and can quote pious platitudes, but how real is Christ to you?

The first thing that Israel did was to bring those old sick cows as sacrifices. Now they are saying, "Oh, this is boring! All these long services. Bible study certainly is boring." I thank God that over a period of twenty-one years, we averaged fifteen hundred people for Bible study in our midweek service in downtown Los Angeles. I have always thanked God for that. But when someone would come and pat me on the back and tell me how wonderful it was, I would remind them of those great office buildings there in downtown Los Angeles. Each afternoon well over two hundred thousand people would empty out of those buildings to go home. Out of that number only about fifteen hundred would return on Thursday nights for Bible study. Our batting average was not really very good, was it? Most of the people who worked in those buildings were church members, and probably they were all out to church on Easter Sunday. They could always make it to the ball game at Dodger Stadium on Sunday afternoon, but they would find it impossible to get to the Sunday evening service. Today there is a great deal of religion, but very little real Christianity. A great many folk are just playing church. When I was a kid, we played store. I used to fill tin cans with dirt and sell them to the other kids in the neighborhood. My, I ran a store! Playing store never got anywhere, but it was a lot of fun. And there are a lot of adults having fun playing church today.

At the time that I was ordained into the ministry, the man who gave me the charge of entering the ministry said that there are three great sins of the ministry that I should avoid. Maybe I haven't followed through as I should, but I have always remembered those three sins.

The number one sin of the ministry is laziness. Yes, that's right. The reason we don't have more expositors of the Word of God today is because it requires study to be an expositor. It is so easy for a pastor to get busy during the week. Shame on you, if you're taking your preacher's time during the week and not letting him study if he wants to study. Any church that has a man who is an expositor and wants to spend time in study should let him study. He needs that time, and he'll have to have it if he's going to be an expositor. He cannot be lazy and expect to be a real teacher of the Word of God.

One young fellow who was a student of mine at Biola became a pastor in California's San Joaquin Valley. After he had been up there about three years, he came down and said he wanted to talk to me. We went to lunch, and I asked him, "What's your problem?"

"I'm getting ready to get out of the ministry. I've run out of things to preach. I'm beginning simply to repeat myself, and people notice it."

So I said, "How long do you take to prepare a sermon?"

"Well, I've preached all of yours that I have. And I've preached others. Generally, I prepare one in three hours."

I told him, "Although my sermons may not look like it, I spent over twenty-four hours just preparing each sermon. I have never preached a sermon until I was ready to preach."

Laziness is a great sin, and I don't think that God excuses it. I dealt with a young fellow recently who wanted to go into the ministry, and at one time he had high hopes of going to seminary. Now he has the vain notion that he can become a preacher by just going out and letting the Holy Spirit teach him. My friend, the Holy Spirit has never yet taught a *lazy* preacher. He will only teach the one who is willing to go all the way in study.

Spiritual worship became wearisome to the people of Israel because they didn't love the Word of God. You have to love the Word of God. This is one way in which the Bible is different from any other book. Any other book you must read before you love it, and you must understand it before you can love it. But, my friend, you must love the Word of God before you can understand it. The Spirit of God is not teaching lazy folk.

Then the *second* great sin of the ministry is an overwhelming ambition. This can manifest itself in several different ways. It's a form of covetousness, of desiring fame, of wanting to be a big preacher, of wanting to preach to the crowd. This is a great sin in the ministry today: wanting to speak to crowds. I am convinced that the great preachers today are not in the big churches, and they are not always the ones getting the big crowds. I listened to a man some time ago preach a sermon, and I do not think there were a hundred people present. But it was a great sermon, an expository sermon. It just thrilled my heart to hear that young man preach. I asked him, "How long did you spend preparing that sermon?" He told me that he had been working on it all week. I suppose that boy put in over twenty hours getting up that message, and he's *willing* to be a pastor to a small group of people. However, too many are eager to become great and to minister to a large church.

I heard the story of a preacher somewhere in Texas who came home and told his wife one day, "The next town over has a church which has asked me if I would consider a call to their church. It's a larger town, a larger church, they pay a larger salary, and they are really lots better people over there. I'm going upstairs to pray about it and to see what the Lord wants me to do."

She said, "I'll go up and pray with you."

"Oh, no," he said, "you stay down here and start packing!" I am afraid that there are a great many in the ministry who are just like that.

The third great sin of the ministry is to be dull and boring, to be tedious and wearisome. The reason this happens, of course, is that a man does not stay enough in the Book. A man doesn't have to have charisma—many do not—but there is no excuse for being apathetic, very prosaic, colorless, and lackluster.

I mentioned earlier that my wife and I went to see *Richard III*. Shakespeare was a great writer. I don't think he just dashed it off, all of a sudden. We are told that he spent hours writing his plays. I listened to the two young men, one of them playing the part of Richard III and the other playing the one who was supposed to have been his friend but who finally dethroned him and put him in the Tower of London. Of course Shakespeare was a genius, but the thing that impressed me about the play above everything else was the way these young men enunciated, how clearly they spoke, and how they had worked on their lines. I watched purposefully because I had been in Shakespearean plays when I was very young. They didn't miss a

cue. There wasn't one slip of the tongue. They went right through it.
Do you know why? They had worked and worked and rehearsed and
rehearsed and rehearsed. If the actor in the world can spend all that
time preparing for a performance, why can't we spend time preparing
to give out the Word of God? Any preacher who goes into the pulpit
unprepared despises the name of the Lord, and he is causing people to
say, "Boy, the Bible is boring! And going to church is tiresome. Next
Sunday I'll do something interesting." Being a dull preacher is another great sin of the ministry.

Verse 14 says, "But cursed be the deceiver, which hath in his flock
a male, and voweth, and sacrificeth unto the Lord a corrupt thing."
Here is something else people do: making vows to God and then not
following through on them. We find it taught both in Leviticus and
Proverbs that God does not want us telling Him something unless we
mean it. If you promise to do something for God, you had better go
through with it because God means business. He doesn't ask you to
make the vow—it is voluntary—but if you make that vow, be sure that
you go through with it.

There were people in Israel who were making great protestations,
saying, "It looks like we're going to have a bumper crop this year. I am
going to give the Lord not only a tenth, but I'm going to give some
freewill offerings to Him." But then when the harvest came in abundance, they decided they would keep it for themselves. They decided
they would not turn it over to the Lord after all. Instead, they offered to
God the corrupt, the lame, and the sick.

CHAPTER 2

THEME: The priests reproved for profanity and the people rebuked for social sins

In this chapter we come to another section, but it is still dealing with the priests. God is reproving the priests for their profanity. They were profane (*fanus* means "temple"); they were against the temple. Instead of serving God, they were opposed to God, disgracing God in the very service they were performing in the temple.

In the first chapter, we saw that the priests were despising God's name, and I mentioned the old sick cows which they presented as an offering to God. The real condemnation of that practice was not because they were giving a valueless thing to God and He was rebuking them because they were not giving as they should. A little later He will come to that and will ask the very pointed question, "Will a man rob God?" But here the emphasis is not upon the *value* of the offering but upon the *character* of the offering that was placed on the altar. In the Book of Leviticus we find that there are five great offerings mentioned, and each of them points to Jesus Christ. Each offering had to represent the One who was coming, and this One was holy, harmless, undefiled, and separate from sinners. He was perfect, and the offering which represented and pointed to Him must be without blemish. The sweet savor and even the nonsweet savor offerings pointed to the Son of God. Now in the days of Malachi the priests were despising God's name in that they were bringing to God an imperfect offering—an old sick cow! It was blasphemy to bring a diseased or crippled animal to the altar as a representation of the perfect One who was coming.

The same thing is being done in our day. A few years ago the very popular rock opera *Jesus Christ, Superstar* presented the Lord Jesus as an immoral, confused man. Well, the world cannot forget Him that's for sure, but the world is not thinking *rightly* of Him. Those who represent Him in books and plays and even in the liberal pulpit are despising the name of God. We hear flippant expressions like "the Devil made me do it." Well, the Devil didn't make you do it; you did it because you have that old sinful nature. Another expression is "God will get you!" No, He won't! Do you think God is running around paddling little boys and girls? Oh, my friend, let's guard against misrepresenting God.

Our God is gracious, and He is to be held in reverence. He does judge sin and will judge sin in the future. He is called the awful God, that is, the awe-inspiring God. He is the reverend God. He is to be respected. He is to be worshiped. He is to be adored.

The other night I was listening to snatches of Bach's music and was struck by the fact that it was nothing in the world but praise to God. We don't have much of pure praise to God even today in our so-called fundamental churches. Our failure to praise God and our praise of men instead is another way in which we despise God's name. This is a condemnation of our contemporary church.

Since all true believers are priests in the age in which we live, this prophecy of Malachi's which is directed to priests has real meaning for us.

In chapter 1, verse 6, God addresses the priests and rebukes them for despising His name. Now in chapter 2, verse 1, He addresses them again—

And now, O ye priests, this commandment is for you [Mal. 2:1].

You see, He is still dealing with the priests.

If ye will not hear, and if ye will not lay it to heart, to give glory unto my name, saith the LORD of hosts, I will even send a curse upon you, and I will curse your blessings: yea, I have cursed them already, because ye do not lay it to heart [Mal. 2:2].

They were not taking their office seriously. And God was going to judge them more severely than he would judge the people. Why? Because of their position of responsibility. They were permitting this sordid condition to exist. They were shutting their eyes to the fact that people were bringing lame and sick animals for sacrifice. God had given them the law of truth, and they were to teach it to their people.

Now I am going to make a very strong statement. I would rather be the worst sinner on this earth—even a gangster or a murderer—than to be a minister who goes into the pulpit with an unbelieving heart and gives only a few little pious platitudes to the congregation. God is certainly going to hold that man responsible.

> **Behold, I will corrupt your seed, and spread dung upon your faces, even the dung of your solemn feasts; and one shall take you away with it [Mal. 2:3].**

"Behold, I will corrupt your seed." Apparently God had been blessing the people, and they had been getting abundant harvests at this time. You will remember that the priests were to be given the tithe of the crops—wheat, barley, figs, grapes—a tenth was given to the Lord to support the priests. Now God says that He will corrupt the seed out there so that they wouldn't be getting the tithe that they had been getting. Their affluent society was about done with.

"And [I will] spread dung upon your faces." The interesting thing was that all the maw of the sacrificial animal was given to the priests, but the dung in the maw was rejected and taken away. It could never be left in the sacrificial animal. Therefore, when God says that He will spread dung upon the faces of the priests, it is as if He is saying that He is going to rub their noses in it. And when that happens, they will not be able to serve at His altar. Why? Because no unclean thing can come there, and they will certainly be unclean! This is strong language that God is using here.

> **And ye shall know that I have sent this commandment unto you, that my covenant might be with Levi, saith the LORD of hosts.**
>
> **My covenant was with him of life and peace; and I gave them to him for the fear wherewith he feared me, and was afraid before my name.**

> **The law of truth was in his mouth, and iniquity was not
> found in his lips: he walked with me in peace and eq-
> uity, and did turn many away from iniquity [Mal.
> 2:4–6].**

This tells us the reason that God chose the tribe of Levi. If we look at
Levi, the son of Jacob, we would never choose him because he had
nothing to commend him to God. And when old Jacob was dying, he
called his twelve sons to stand around his bedside, and he gave a
prophecy, which we find in Genesis 49, concerning each of them. He
combined Simeon and Levi into one prophecy: "Simeon and Levi are
brethren; instruments of cruelty are in their habitations. O my soul,
come not thou into their secret; unto their assembly, mine honour, be
not thou united: for in their anger they slew a man, and in their
selfwill they digged down a wall." They felt justified in doing it because their sister had been raped, but they were murderers. Jacob's
prophecy continues: "Cursed be their anger, for it was fierce; and
their wrath, for it was cruel: I will divide them in Jacob, and scatter
them in Israel" (Gen. 49:5–7).

How was God going to scatter Levi in Israel? They would become
the priestly tribe. They didn't get any territory of the land but were
scattered among the tribes. But how could they become the priestly
tribe when Levi himself was such a rascal and a murderer? We need to
follow along in history to see why God chose the tribe of Levi.

Centuries later, when the children of Israel went into idolatry and
made the golden calf to worship, Moses called for the idolaters to be
slain. It was the tribe of Levi who did according to the word of Moses.
When Moses was about to die, he gathered the tribes around him. The
twelve sons of Jacob had become more than a million people who were
gathered around Moses. Now Moses gives a prophecy to each of the
tribes, and this is his blessing on Levi: ". . . Let thy Thummim and the
Urim be with thy holy one, whom thou didst prove at Massah, and
with whom thou didst strive at the waters of Meribah; who said unto
his father and to his mother, I have not seen him; neither did he acknowledge his brethren, nor knew his own children: for they have
observed thy word, and kept thy covenant. They shall teach Jacob thy

judgments, and Israel thy law: they shall put incense before thee, and whole burnt sacrifice upon thine altar" (Deut. 33:8–10).

Notice that although Levi himself was a brutal murderer, the tribe that came from him observed the Word of God; they kept His covenant. And God made them the priestly tribe to teach the people of Israel the law of God and to offer prayers and sacrifices before Him— those sacrifices pointed to Christ. Therefore, "Bless, LORD, his substance, and accept the work of his hands: smite through the loins of them that rise against him, and of them that hate him, that they rise not again" (Deut. 33:11).

That is the covenant which God made with the tribe of Levi. He was to teach Israel, he was to serve at the place of prayer, the altar of incense, and he was to offer the burnt sacrifices which point to Christ. When we move forward in history to the time of Malachi and the remnant which had returned to the land of Israel after the Babylonian captivity, what is the tribe of Levi like? Well, we have seen that he is willing to shut his eyes when a sick cow is brought as a sacrifice to God. He is despising the name of God, and he is disobeying God. Therefore, how can he teach God's Word to the people? What a change has taken place! Even after the seventy-year captivity, Levi hasn't learned the lesson. "My covenant was with him of life and peace; and I gave them to him for the fear wherewith he feared me, and was afraid before my name." God is saying through Malachi that Levi previously feared Him, but now the tribe doesn't. "The law of truth was in his mouth." He had taught the truth of God. But these priests are not only failing to teach the truth of God, they also are breaking the commandments of God. He continues, "The law of truth was in his mouth, and iniquity was not found in his lips: he walked with me in peace and equity, and did turn many away from iniquity." He had been a good example, you see, to the people. What a change has taken place.

There is a real application in this for us today. No one can serve God without a reverence for His name. That means that Christ must be lifted up before the people. If Christ is lifted up, He will draw men to Himself. He is lifted up by our witness, and that must be by our lives as well as by our words. Our example is just as important as what we say.

> **For the priest's lips should keep knowledge, and they should seek the law at his mouth: for he is the messenger of the LORD of hosts [Mal. 2:7].**

The priests are to be messengers of the Lord of hosts. The word *messenger*, as I have pointed out before, is also translated "angel," and in the Book of Revelation we find the Lord addressing the "angel" of the church of Ephesus, etc. To whom is He speaking? He is addressing the one who is the leader of the church, the one who is teaching the Word of God in the church.

Now let me sum this up by giving my interpretation of this—and you may not agree with it. I believe that the sole duty of the pastor of a church is to *teach* the Word of God. God have mercy on the church that expects its pastor to be the public relations man, running all over the countryside visiting sick babies and burping them, and expects him to spend his time in the administration of church affairs when he should be studying the Word of God and then teaching it to his people.

Once I had a telephone call from a man back east who was an officer in his church and was dissatisfied with his pastor. He said that his pastor spent his time studying instead of administering the affairs of the church. So I asked him, "Did you tell me that you are a deacon?"

"Yes."

"Have you yourself been visiting the sick?"

"No, sir, I keep pretty busy."

"Do you know that that is your business? *You* are to visit the sick. You are to take charge of the administration of the church. His business is to teach the Word of God. If he is not teaching the Word of God when he gets into the pulpit, that is another story. But if he is spending his time in studying and giving out God's Word, then he is doing what God has called him to do."

Remember that a situation like this confronted the apostles in the early church. The Hellenistic Jews were complaining that their widows were being neglected and preference was being given to the native-born widows. The matter was brought before the apostles, and they did a marvelous job of handling it. They told the church to appoint deacons to handle it. They said, ". . . It is not reason that we should leave the word of God, and serve tables" (Acts 6:2).

Having completed my ministry in the church, I stand at a great vantage point today. I thank God that I have reached the place where I no longer have to burp babies and, although I have a little to do with administration, that is not how I spend my time. I am currently spending more time in the study of the Word than ever before, and I thank God for it. If I could relive my days as a pastor, I would spend more time studying the Word—some folk thought I spent too much time as it was. But I believe that studying the Word and teaching it is the pastor's business.

God says that it was Levi's business, but in Malachi's day the priests were not doing it. Therefore, God says to the priests,

> **But ye are departed out of the way; ye have caused many to stumble at the law; ye have corrupted the covenant of Levi, saith the LORD of hosts.**

> **Therefore have I also made you contemptible and base before all the people, according as ye have not kept my ways, but have been partial in the law [Mal. 2:8–9].**

There was a time in our own land when ministers were listened to, but that day is past. God said this would happen when the ministry is not giving out His Word.

> **Have we not all one father? hath not one God created us? why do we deal treacherously every man against his brother, by profaning the covenant of our fathers? [Mal. 2:10].**

"Have we not all one father?" There are some expositors who say that the "father" refers to Abraham since both Israel and Judah are mentioned in the verse that follows. However, I think that the next question makes it clear that Malachi is speaking about God as the Father: "Hath not one God created us?"

He also makes it clear in what way God is the Father. He is the Father by creation. But man lost that relationship. Adam was called the son of God, but after the Fall, he begat a son in his own likeness—not in the likeness of God, but in the likeness of his own fallen nature. Therefore, when the nation Israel comes into view, we do not find God speaking specifically of any individual Israelite as His son. Rather, He speaks of the corporate body of the nation as a son. Never in the Old Testament does God refer to an individual as His son. Even of two men who were outstanding, Moses and David, it was "Moses my *servant*" and "David my *servant*." Never does God say, "Moses my *son*" or "David my *son*." Individuals become sons of God through faith in Jesus Christ. God is the Father of mankind in the sense that He is the Creator.

This is something that has been greatly emphasized in our contemporary society, and I think properly so. On a telecast I heard a man, who was definitely an unsaved man, play up the fact that we are all human beings and that we ought to show respect and consideration for one another. Well, that is true. As far as he went, he was entirely accurate. You are a human being and I am a human being, and I should accord to you the same rights and privileges and respect that I would like to have for myself. "Have we not all one father? hath not one God created us?" We all are the creation of God.

"Why do we deal treacherously every man against his brother, by profaning the covenant of our fathers?" Now here they were, a chosen people, yet breaking God's covenant and dealing treacherously one with the other. They were not right with God, and so they were not right with each other.

This is certainly true of man in our day. I personally have to say that there are a great many unsaved people that I wouldn't trust. And, unfortunately, having been in the church most of my life, I have to say that there are a lot in the church whom I would not trust either. I have no confidence in them at all. Why? They deal treacherously. There is nothing that hurts the cause of Christ more than a church fight, conflicts in the church, and leaders who are at each other's throats. Regardless of how evangelistic a church may be, its witness is nil when those conditions exist.

THE SINS OF DIVORCE AND REMARRIAGE

Judah hath dealt treacherously, and an abomination is committed in Israel and in Jerusalem; for Judah hath profaned the holiness of the LORD which he loved, and hath married the daughter of a strange god [Mal. 2:11].

He is very specific now: "*Judah* hath dealt treacherously, and an abomination is committed in *Israel* and in Jerusalem." Now we know whom Malachi is talking about: "Judah" is the tribe of Judah, "Israel" includes all the twelve tribes, and "Jerusalem" is the capital.

"An abomination is committed in Israel and in Jerusalem." God is talking about how they profane the covenant of the fathers by dealing treacherously with one another. They are profaning the holiness of the Lord. God is holy, and God loves holiness. God doesn't love sin; He hates sin. Now God will spell it out to them. He specifically tells them what He is talking about (see Gen. 6:1–7).

"And hath married the daughter of a strange [foreign] god." The men saw the beautiful foreign girls who lived around them when they returned from the Captivity. So they were leaving their wives and marrying these foreign girls who served heathen, pagan deities, and brought idolatry into the nation.

We see this same thing all the way through the Word of God. I believe this is the situation in Genesis 6:1–7 where we are told that the sons of God were marrying the daughters of men. I certainly do not hold the view of some expositors that the "sons of God" were angels who were cohabitating with human women and producing some sort of monstrous offspring. Our Lord expressly said that angels do not marry (Matt. 22:30). Rather, this marks the beginning of the breaking down of the godly line of Seth as they intermarried with the ungodly line of Cain.

We see this happening again when the children of Israel were nearing the Promised Land. The king of Moab hired Balaam to curse Israel because the Moabites feared them. When God would not permit Balaam to curse them, he gave the king of Moab some very bad advice— bad for Israel. He said to let the daughters of Moab marry the sons of

Israel. They did intermarry, and this brought the idolatry of Moab into Israel.

Again after the kingdom of Israel was divided, the idolatry of Phoenecia was introduced into the northern kingdom by the marriage of Ahab with Jezebel, the daughter of Ethbaal, who was first an idolatrous priest, then king of Tyre and Sidon.

Now this was happening again in Malachi's day. We learn from Nehemiah that there were all kinds of pagan people living around the returned remnant. A young Israelite would see some good-looking foreign girl and decide that he would like to have her for a wife. So he would get rid of his own Israelite wife and marry this pagan girl.

It is the same old story that is being reenacted in our day. I have been sounding a warning here in Southern California since 1940, but the divorce rate keeps climbing. Nobody is paying any attention to me, but I'll keep on saying that a believer and an unbeliever ought not to get married. Any girl or any boy who flies in the face of God's very definite and specific instructions in this connection is just flirting with trouble. Believe me, problems will be coming their way. It cannot be otherwise.

> The LORD will cut off the man that doeth this, the master
> and the scholar, out of the tabernacles of Jacob, and him
> that offereth an offering unto the LORD of hosts [Mal.
> 2:12].

"The LORD will cut off the man that doeth this, the master and the scholar." It doesn't make any difference who he is, he will suffer the same judgment. "And him that offereth an offering unto the LORD of hosts." Neither will he escape if he goes through the temple ritual but continues to live in sin.

My friend, a true child of God will not continue to live in sin. That is the reason the prodigal son down there in the pigpen finally came to himself and said, "I will arise and go to my father . . ." (Luke 15:18). He was a son and not a pig. He had the nature of his father and could not continue to live as a pig.

I received a startling letter from a church officer here in Southern

California who asked for help because he "couldn't give up the awful sin of adultery." If he is a child of God, he will get out of the pigpen. Nothing but pigs love the pigpen and are satisfied to stay down there. A son will get out of it.

> **And this have ye done again, covering the altar of the LORD with tears, with weeping, and with crying out, insomuch that he regardeth not the offering any more, or receiveth it with good will at your hand [Mal. 2:13].**

The wives of these men who were divorcing them and marrying foreign girls came to the altar weeping. They shed their tears upon the altar, and God said, "I heard them. Then later you came along very piously and placed your offering upon the same altar on which were the tears of your wives! I want you to know that I paid no attention to your offering."

The church officer who wrote me the letter (to which I referred earlier) may be the treasurer of the church or the head deacon. I can assure him that God is paying no attention to his "good works." In fact, it would be better if he stayed at home and kept out of sight. God makes it very clear that He "regardeth not the offering any more, or receiveth it with good will at your hand." He knows your hypocrisy and will not accept your service.

Now the men in Malachi's day, with feigned innocence and pretended ignorance, ask why—

> **Yet ye say, Wherefore? Because the LORD hath been witness between thee and the wife of thy youth, against whom thou hast dealt treacherously: yet is she thy companion, and the wife of thy covenant [Mal. 2:14].**

"Yet ye say, Wherefore?" God is offensive even to suggest that He wouldn't accept their offering. The thought is that they were saying, "Why wouldn't He accept it? I brought a very nice fat lamb to offer." When they ask the question, Malachi spells out the answer for them in neon lights so they cannot misunderstand Him—"Because the LORD hath been witness between thee and the wife of thy youth, against whom thou hast dealt treacherously." You see, the Israelite married a Hebrew girl when he was a young man. But when he grew older and moved among the pagan and heathen about him, he decided that he wanted to marry a pagan with whom he had gotten acquainted.

"Yet is she thy companion, and the wife of thy covenant." His Hebrew wife was the one with whom he stood before the priest and covenanted to be faithful and true to her.

The next verse has always been a difficult passage to interpret, but it is my feeling that Dr. Charles Feinberg is accurate when in his book, *The Minor Prophets*, he says that the natural interpretation is that the prophet is speaking of divorce. And the reference is to the original institution of marriage by God Himself.

> **And did not he make one? Yet had he the residue of the spirit. And wherefore one? That he might seek a godly seed. Therefore take heed to your spirit, and let none deal treacherously against the wife of his youth [Mal. 2:15].**

"And did not he make one?" goes back to the original creation of man and woman. Adam was a half and Eve was a half, and together they made one. This is evident when a child is born—he is part of both parents. The two are certainly one in the child.

"Yet had he the residue of the spirit. And wherefore [why] one? That he might seek a godly seed." You see, she is to be like he is—spiritually as well as physically for the sake of the family. A home where there is divorce or where there is polygamy is not a fit place in which to raise children.

My friend, if you are a young lady, you ought not marry that young man unless he believes as you do because, actually, you are supposed to go his way. And you are going to find the going rough if you are a child of God and he is not.

If you are a young man or a young woman, let me say this to you. If you think that you can win your sweetheart to Christ, make sure that you do it *before* your marriage because that is when you have the greatest influence. I tell you, a young fellow in love will do almost anything to please the girl he wants to marry. But after marriage he will not be anxious to please her. And, of course, that holds true for a young woman in love also. If you don't win your sweetheart to Christ before marriage, you are in trouble, and I mean deep trouble.

"Therefore take heed to your spirit, and let none deal treacherously against the wife of his youth." Malachi is warning them to watch what they are doing. God had specifically forbidden His people to inter-marry with the heathen.

You may remember that Nehemiah, after he had built the walls of Jerusalem, had returned to his job as the king's cupbearer down in the capital of Media–Persia. But after he had been there for awhile, he got a vacation and came back to Jerusalem. He found that old Tobiah, an Ammonite, an enemy of God, had been moved into an apartment in the temple! The high priest had made this arrangement for him be-cause his son had married the daughter of Tobiah. Do you know what Nehemiah did about it? He went over there and pitched out all of To-biah's belongings, even the furniture, and told him to take off. You may think that is pretty rough and certainly not very polite. No, it wasn't polite, but it sure did cleanse the temple! As a matter of fact, Nehemiah was pretty rough with his own people whom he found had intermarried with the pagans of Ashdod, of Ammon, and of Moab. Nehemiah himself records his treatment of them: "And I contended with them, and cursed them, and smote certain of them, and plucked off their hair, and made them swear by God, saying, Ye shall not give your daughters unto their sons, nor take their daughters unto your sons, or for yourselves" (Neh. 13:25). And he reminded them of the disaster which had come to their nation through intermarriage with the heathen. Oh, how we need laymen like Nehemiah in our day to stand for the Word of God!

> **For the LORD, the God of Israel, saith that he hateth put-ting away: for one covereth violence with his garment, saith the LORD of hosts: therefore take heed to your spirit, that ye deal not treacherously [Mal. 2:16].**

In the Old Testament, when a man married a girl, he took his garment, his outer garment, and put it over her. This lovely custom was to signify that he was going to protect her.

This was the lovely thing which Boaz did for Ruth. Ruth was a widow and, according to the Mosaic Law, she had to claim Boaz as her kinsman–redeemer before he could act. He could not ask her to marry him; she had to claim him. So Naomi, acting like a regular matchmaker, sent Ruth down to the threshing floor. It was harvest time, and all the families were camped around the threshing floor. At night, to protect the grain, the men slept around it with their heads toward the heap of grain and their feet stuck out like spokes of a wheel. Ruth followed Naomi's instructions and laid at the feet of Boaz. When he realized that someone was there and asked who it was, she replied, ". . . I am Ruth thine handmaid: spread therefore thy skirt over thine handmaid; for thou hast a near kinsman" (Ruth 3:9). She was asking him to put his cloak over her, asking for his protection as her kinsman–redeemer—in other words, asking him to marry her. In marriage a man offers a woman his protection and his love.And she offers her devotion and her life to him. This is a beautiful picture of Christ's relationship with believers.

In Malachi's day the men of Israel were dealing treacherously with their wives. They had covered them with their garments in marriage, but now they were covering their garment with violence. In other words, they had divorced their wives.

Notice that God says that He *hates* divorce—"the LORD, the God of Israel, saith that he hateth putting away."

God's ideal for man from the very beginning was that there should be no divorce. We know that, because Jesus said that Moses allowed divorce because of the hardness of men's hearts but that from the beginning it was not so. Then how was it at the beginning? "And Adam gave names to all cattle, and to the fowl of the air, and to every beast of the field; but for Adam there was not found an help meet for him" (Gen. 2:20). To begin with, we learn that among all the creation of God that was beneath man, none could take the place of what God would create for Adam, that is, a wife. God had created all other creatures by twos. Neither could man find a mate from the angels which were created above man. So man was pretty much alone. God let Adam give names to all the animals so that Adam would discover for himself that he was alone and that he needed somebody there with him. Only half of him had really been created at the beginning. He needed somebody like he was and yet different from him. He needed one who was a help "meet" or fit for him. He needed someone to be fitted to him. He was just a half, and he needed the other half to be put there so that together they could be one. That was the thing God had in mind. God created Adam first and allowed him time to realize that he needed someone else.

I really get provoked when I hear people talk as if sex is something that is bad. Of course, the sex act outside of marriage is wrong. But after all, who was it that thought of sex? God is the One who thought of it and made it. He is the One who designated man and woman. He had in mind a marvelous arrangement when He created the sexes.

"And the LORD God caused a deep sleep to fall upon Adam, and he slept: and he took one of his ribs, and closed up the flesh instead thereof" (Gen. 2:21). Why did God do that? Why didn't he take her from the ground as He had done with Adam? Because she was to be like Adam and yet different from him. She must come from man because man is not really a whole person. She was made from his side. This is not some foolish story. God wants to impress upon man that woman is part of man, that he is only half a man without a woman.

It has been said that God did not take Eve from Adam's head so that she should be his superior. Neither did He take Eve from his foot to be his servant. He took Eve from Adam's side to be his equal and to be his companion. She came from near his heart so that he would love her. She is to be his helper. Together they become one. One plus one equals one. That is God's arithmetic, and that is accurate.

The Scripture knows nothing about this idea of either women's lib or the other extreme, the inferiority of women. God put woman on a high plane. It is obvious to us already that the people in the days of Malachi had lost that vision. That is why God was reminding them, "When you sin against the wife of your youth, you are sinning against Me." God protects the status of women.

"And the rib, which the LORD God had taken from man, made he a

woman, and brought her unto the man" (Gen. 2:22). She must have
been a beautiful creation. God brought her and gave her unto the man.
Certainly God made that marriage. The institution of marriage was
made in heaven. God's intention was for marriage to be a blessing.
God blessed it, and He intended for it to work for man's benefit.

"And Adam said, This is now bone of my bones, and flesh of my
flesh: she shall be called Woman, because she was taken out of Man"
(Gen. 2:23). What is woman? Adam was ish, and woman is ishah. She
is the other side or other half of the male. We call them male and female. She is "bone of my bones and flesh of my flesh." She is called
woman because she was taken out of man.

"Therefore shall a man leave his father and his mother, and shall
cleave unto his wife: and they shall be one flesh" (Gen. 2:24). This
excommunicates mothers-in-law and fathers-in-law. This removes
them from the new family. I'm afraid a great many folk today do not
get the right instruction about marriage. A marriage establishes a new
creation. Papa and Mamma are not a part of the new creation. The
young couple has left them. And they, the man and wife, shall be one
flesh.

"And they were both naked, the man and his wife, and were not
ashamed" (Gen. 2:25). This was before sin had entered into the world.
Neither one looked with lust upon the other because at that time they
were innocent. They looked upon each other with tenderness and
with love. There was a mutual respect. Each of them could truly say,
"You are the one for me." The creation of Eve made Adam a man, all
man. The presence of Adam made Eve a woman, all woman.

Then sin entered into the world. It marred everything, including
the relationship in marriage. When we get to the time of Moses and
the Law, we find that divorce was permitted. This does not mean that it
was God's intention when He instituted marriage, but He permitted it,
as Jesus said, because of the hardness of man's heart. The Mosaic Law
said this: "When a man hath taken a wife, and married her, and it
come to pass that she find no favour in his eyes, because he hath found
some uncleanness in her: then let him write her a bill of divorcement,
and give it in her hand, and send her out of his house" (Deut. 24:1).
"Uncleanness" in the bride implies that her husband found that she

was not a virgin; then he could write her a bill of divorcement. She had deceived her husband by not being what she claimed to be. He had been "taken in" by her. Naturally, this would lead to trouble in the home, and lead to fighting later on.

By the time of the New Testament, the interpretation of "uncleanness" had become so broad that if a wife even burned the biscuits, that would be grounds for divorce. When Jesus was asked the question, "Is it lawful for a man to put away his wife for every cause?" the rabbis were teaching that a wife could be divorced upon the slightest whim, which was certainly contrary to the intent of the Mosaic Law.

There were other specifics in this Mosaic Law: "And when she is departed out of his house, she may go and be another man's wife. And if the latter husband hate her, and write her a bill of divorcement, and giveth it in her hand, and sendeth her out of his house; or if the latter husband die, which took her to be his wife; her former husband, which sent her away, may not take her again to be his wife, after that she is defiled; for that is abomination before the LORD: and thou shalt not cause the land to sin, which the LORD thy God giveth thee for an inheritance" (Deut. 24:2-4). That would be progressive prostitution, and it would lead to the sort of thing we are seeing in our contemporary society, to people being married and divorced seven or eight times! To do that is absolutely to ridicule the marriage vow.

The problem that was prevelant in Israel at the time of Malachi is prevalent in our contemporary culture today. We have certainly changed our viewpoint on divorce in recent years in this country. I suppose that divorce is one of the most controversial subjects that any Bible teacher has to discuss today because there is confusion as to what the Bible really says on that problem, and there is a great difference and wide diversion of interpretation. If I may use the colloquialism of the street—it is a hot potato. You cannot say that there are no grounds for divorce, although that was the unanimous decision of the church one hundred years ago—in spite of what the Word of God had to say.

The Lord Jesus made two things very clear on this subject of divorce: (1) Moses had permitted divorce because of the hardness of heart of the people; and (2) there is one clear-cut basis for divorce—

that is fornication, unfaithfulness on the part of either the man or the woman. Notice this record in Matthew's Gospel: "The Pharisee also came unto him, tempting him, and saying unto him, Is it lawful for a man to put away his wife for every cause? And he answered and said unto them, Have ye not read, that he which made them at the beginning made them male and female, and said, For this cause shall a man leave father and mother, and shall cleave to his wife: and they twain shall be one flesh?" (Matt. 19:3–5).

As I mentioned before, Jesus goes back to the beginning, to the time of creation, when God instituted marriage. "Wherefore they are no more twain, but one flesh. What therefore God hath joined together, let no man put asunder. They say unto him, Why did Moses then command to give a writing of divorcement, and to put her away? He saith unto them, Moses because of the hardness of your hearts suffered you to put away your wives: but from the beginning it was not so" (Matt. 19:6–8).

Then He sets down the reason for which divorce is allowed: "And I say unto you, Whosoever shall put away his wife, except it be for fornication, and shall marry another, committeth adultery: and whoso marrieth her which is put away doth commit adultery" (Matt. 19:9).

It is quite interesting how the disciples followed up that statement with a question: "His disciples say unto him, If the case of the man be so with his wife, it is not good to marry" (Matt. 19:10). In other words, "If it is really that strict, if there is one and only one reason for divorce, then it would be better not to get married at all."

Then our Lord explained the liberty that we have: "But he said unto them, All men cannot receive this saying, save they to whom it is given. For there are some eunuchs, which were so born from their mother's womb: and there are some eunuchs, which were made eunuchs of men: and there be eunuchs, which have made themselves eunuchs for the kingdom of heaven's sake. He that is able to receive it, let him receive it" (Matt. 19:11–12). It is not necessary for everyone to get married. There are some men and some women who do not need to marry. By no means is it a sin to be single. Some folk simply do not need to get married—they are eunuchs from birth. Others are made eunuchs by man, such as Daniel in the court of Nebuchadnezzar. It was forced upon them and served the purpose of making captives more docile toward the king, and it also enabled them to devote more time to their studies. Then there are eunuchs for the Kingdom of Heaven's sake. There are men who have kept themselves eunuchs in order to serve the cause of Christ and the cause of the church. It is wonderful if a man or a woman feels able to do that. I have known several preachers who have never married. I thought I would do the same in my ministry and decided that I would be an old bachelor all my life. But I soon learned that bachelorhood wasn't for me. This is an area in which God has given us great liberty. But the important thing is this: Christ said that if you do choose to get married, it is a lifelong commitment. The only ground for divorce is fornication by your mate.

In the days of the early church this matter of fornication arose in the Corinthian church. People of different religious backgrounds were in the church, and there were couples who had married when they were pagans, then one of the spouses became a Christian. What should be their relationship after one of them became converted? Paul addresses himself to this new situation: "And unto the married I command, yet not I, but the Lord, Let not the wife depart from her husband: but and if she depart, let her remain unmarried, or be reconciled to her husband: and let not the husband put away his wife" (1 Cor. 7:10–11). If a couple had been married when they were pagans and now one is converted to Christianity, the Christian is not to walk out on the marriage. If the believer departs, he is to remain unmarried or else be reconciled again.

"But to the rest speak I, not the Lord: If any brother hath a wife that believeth not, and she be pleased to dwell with him, let him not put her away. And the woman which hath an husband that believeth not, and if he be pleased to dwell with her, let her not leave him. For the unbelieving husband is sanctified by the wife, and the unbelieving wife is sanctified by the husband: else were your children unclean; but now are they holy. But if the unbelieving depart, let him depart. A brother or a sister is not under bondage in such cases: but God hath called us to peace" (1 Cor. 7:12–15). Although Jesus said that fornication was the only cause for divorce, the pagan member of a marriage may want to walk out on the marriage. After the partner becomes a believer, the pagan party man say, "I don't like this arrangement. Things are different now from when I married you. I'm going to leave." In such a case Paul says to let the unbeliever go. Whether the unbeliever goes out and gets married again or not, in this situation I assume it would mean that the believing husband or wife would be free to marry again.

When Paul said, "A brother or a sister is not under bondage in such cases," what is the *bondage?* It is the marriage vows.

When he says, "God hath called us to peace," I believe he is saying that God does not ask any man or woman to live in a *hell* at home. Never. If they find that they cannot get along together, that they fight like cats and dogs, I think that they ought to separate. On several occasions I have advised couples to separate—but neither of them is to remarry. Their problem is not divorce, it is marriage. They should not have married in the first place. God has called us to peace; therefore the home is not to be a boxing ring. It is not a place for karate; it is a place for *love.*

A home of love is God's ideal for man. From the beginning God did not intend to have divorce, but, because of man's sin, He permitted it. You may say, "Well, divorce is sinful." Sure it is, and so is murder. But a murderer can be saved. In fact, one was dying on a cross next to Jesus, and he got saved. When Jesus Christ died on the Cross, He died for all sins. The thief on the cross was both a thief and a murderer, and his faith in the Lord Jesus Christ and His shed blood saved him. A thief can be saved, and a divorced person can be saved, too. So let's not put divorce in a special category all by itself. If an unsaved person has been a thief and then repents and gets saved by coming to Jesus Christ, he is forgiven for his thievery. We would permit such a man to get married. We would do the same for a murderer. Then let us be fair about divorce. There are people who get divorced before they are saved. When they come to the Lord Jesus Christ, they are forgiven for that sin. I think such a person is free to marry again, and I feel that this is implied in the Scriptures.

Now as an addendum to this important section on marriage and divorce, I would like to look at it from a little different viewpoint by including a message which I have entitled *The Best Love* (which is also available in booklet form).

THE BEST LOVE

There is an obsession with sex today that is positively frightening and absolutely alarming! You need only consult contemporary literature to recognize this. In a leading British paper some time ago, this statement was made: "Popular morality is now a wasteland, littered with the debris of broken convictions." And it was Judge Barron of the Superior Court of Massachusetts who said, "At too many colleges today, sexual promiscuity among students is a dangerous and growing evil." The Billy Graham paper, *Decision*, had an editorial (I suppose it was way back in 1964) on the church and the moral crisis in which there is this quotation: "So our young people go riding down the highroad to hell in an atmosphere that would make any self-respecting animal sick to its stomach, and no one thinks that matters are as bad as they seem." That is a tremendous statement. An outstanding Christian writer in America says, "But where are the compelling external cries to match the inner voices of the soul which at times murmur darkly and other times shout clamourously that all is not well, that wayward feet are treading the way of wrath, the path of judgment?" Then he goes on to say, "The answer is not simply in passing more laws. It is to be found in regeneration by His Spirit, who alone can set men's souls on fire with a divinely sent thirst for greater purity, both for the individual and for the body politic. Apart from such spiritual burning and purging, men sink beneath the weight and corruption of their own sin." These quotations go back to about 1965. But there are other voices being lifted in alarm.

Yet all about us are the advocates of this erotic cult that falsely claim that all of this emphasis on sex is a signal of a new, broad-minded and enlightened era. The facts are that there is nothing new about it. Furthermore, it does not mark the entrance to abundant living. On the contrary, it has characterized the demise of all decadent and decaying civilizations—Egypt, Babylon, Greece, and Rome to name but a few. The sex symbol marks the decline and fall of many a great and noble people. It is part of the death rattle of a fading nation. The French Revolution marked the departure of the glory of France, and it was during that time that a prostitute was placed on an altar and worshiped.

The excuse for paying this abnormal attention to the subject, given by these purveyors of filth and licentiousness, is that a blue-nosed generation of the past put the lid down on it. The false charge is made that the Bible and the church have frowned upon the subject of sex until it is taboo today and can only be whispered of in secret. They go on to place the blame for present-day marriage failures and the increase in divorce on the gross ignorance of young people. "If only they knew more about this fascinating subject," they counsel, "there would be success in marriage." It is true that the Puritans were blue-nosed, and they probably were a little extreme. I would certainly agree with that, and I would not want to go back to that period. But the tragedy of it is that this present generation hasn't found the solution either. After all, the Bible doesn't go with either crowd. I do not think that the Puritans had a Bible basis for their beliefs in this area. Who was it that thought of sex? This crowd in Hollywood thinks that they originated it. God is the One who started all of this, my friend, and He wanted it put on a holy basis.

This modern crowd also plays upon the fact that we Americans do not like censorship, and therefore they should be free to say and publish what they choose. Well, these modern Pied Pipers of Hamlin are leading the younger generation into a moral morass of debauchery with dirty sex books and pornographic literature. They give the impression that you must be knowledgeable of this lascivious and salacious propaganda in order to be sophisticated and suave and sharp. The bible of this group is *Playboy* magazine. These filthy dreamers have flooded the marketplace and the schoolroom today with this smut and depravity—so much so that a modern father said, "It is not how much shall I tell my son, but how much does he know that *I* don't know!" In spite of all this new emphasis on sex, the divorce courts continue to grind out their monotonous story of the tragedy of modern marriage in ever increasing numbers.

Now a knowledge of the physical may have its place in preparation for a happy marriage, but it is inadequate per se to make a happy home, and it gives a perverted and abnormal emphasis which does not belong there. As Dan Bennett said, "One of the troubles with the world is that people mistake sex for love, money for brains, and transistor radios for civilization." That is the problem of the hour.

The Word of God treats the subject of sex with boldness, frankness, and directness. It is not handled as a dirty subject, and it is not taboo nor theoretical, but it is plain and theological. The Bible is straightforward, and it deals with it in high and lofty language. This is the reason we are spending time on this subject here in Malachi. God lays it on the line to these people that this is part of the reason they went into captivity, and it is part of the reason they have been scattered. I think it is time that God is heard. I feel that the pulpit is long overdue in presenting what God has to say on this subject, but it should be kept on the right plane.

In the very beginning it was *God* who created them male and female. It was *God* who brought the woman to the man. And I would like to add this: He did not need to give Adam a lecture on the birds and bees. God blessed them, and marriage became sacred and holy and pure. And, my friend, it is the only relationship among men and women that God does bless down here—He promises to bless no other. He says that if marriage is made according to *His* plan, He will bless it, and there will be happiness.

God *wants* His children to be happily married. He has a plan and purpose for every one of us if we would only listen to Him. The Lord Jesus says to the church at Ephesus, "Nevertheless I have somewhat against thee, because thou hast left thy first love" (Rev. 2:4). Yet the church in Ephesus is the church at its best. The church has never been on a higher spiritual level since then. It is difficult for us in this cold day of apostasy to conceive of the lofty plane to which the Holy Spirit had brought the early church in its personal relationship to Christ. The believers in the early church were *in love with* Christ. They loved Him! And five million of them sealed that love with their own blood by dying as martyrs for Him.

I would like to make a couple of changes in the translation of Revelation 2:4. The word for "first love" is *protan* in the Greek. It means actually the "best." It is the same word our Lord used in the parable of the prodigal son where the father put on the son the *protan* robe—that is, the "best" robe. And to the Ephesian believers Christ is talking about the *best* love. To this church on its high plane, into which a coolness was creeping, Christ says, "Nevertheless I have against thee that thou art leaving [not *had* left] the best love."

Salvation is a love affair. The question that the Lord asks all of us is, "Do you love Me?" He is not asking, "Are you going to be faithful?" or "Are you going to the mission field?" He is not asking "How much are you going to give?" or "How much are you going to do?" He is asking "Do you love Me?" Then He will tell you that you are to obey Him and that there will be something for you to do. The apostle John put it like this: "We love him, because he first loved us" (1 John 4:19). The second book I ever wrote was on the little Book of Ruth. My reason for writing it was to show that redemption is a romance. God took the lives of two ordinary people, a very strong and virile man and a very beautiful and noble woman, and he told their love story. In that story God revealed to man His great love for him. It was a way to get this amazing fact through to us: Salvation is a love affair.

In Christ's last letter to the Ephesian church in the Book of the Revelation, He sounds a warning. We do not quite understand this. But I go back thirty or forty years to His first letter to these believers, written through Paul. We call it the Epistle of Paul to the Ephesians. In this epistle He discussed this matter of marital love and compared it to the love of Christ for the church. This has been one of the most misunderstood passages in the Word of God. Listen: "Wives, submit yourselves unto your own husbands, as unto the Lord" (Eph. 5:22). There has been natural resentment against this on the part of some, especially very dominant women, for many years. And the women's liberation movement would oppose it. But to resent this is to miss the meaning that is here. Submission is actually for the purpose of headship in the home. It is not a question of one lording it over the other; it is headship for the purpose of bringing order into the home.

But in addition to this it reveals something else that is quite wonderful. He says, "For the husband is the head of the wife, even as Christ is the head of the church: and he is the saviour of the body" (Eph. 5:23). The analogy, you see, is to Christ and the church. Christian marriage down here, if it is made under the Lord, is a miniature of the relationship of Christ and the church. Christian marriage is an adumbration of that wonderful relationship between Christ and the believer. Christian marriage and the relationship of Christ and the church are sacred.

Now will you listen to me very carefully. The physical act of marriage is sacred. It is a religious ritual. It is a sacrament. I do not mean a sacrament made by a church, nor is it made by a man-made ceremony. But it is a sacrement that is made by God Himself, one which He sanctifies, and He says that this relationship is to reveal to you the love of Christ for your soul. Therefore, the woman is to see in a man one to whom she can yield herself in glorious abandonment. She can give herself wholly and completely and find perfect fulfillment and satisfaction in this man, because this is the man for her.

She delights in her husband, in his person, his character, his affection; to her he is not only the chief and foremost of mankind, but in her eyes he is all in all. Her heart's love belongs to him, and to him only. He is her little world, her Paradise, her choice treasure. She is glad to sink her individuality in his. She seeks no renown for herself; his honor is reflected upon her, and she rejoices in it. She will defend his name with her dying breath; safe enough is he where she can speak of him. His smiling gratitude is all the reward she seeks. Even in her dress she thinks of him and considers nothing beautiful which is distasteful to him. He has many objects in life, some of which she does not quite understand; but she believes in them all, and anything she can do to promote them she delights to perform. . . . Such a wife, as a true spouse, realizes the model marriage relation and sets forth what our oneness with the Lord ought to be (Richard Ellsworth Day, *The Shadow of the Broad Brim*, p. 104).

My beloved, that is a marvelous picture of the wife in a real Christian marriage. The man is to see in the woman one he can worship. Some-one says, "Do you mean worship?" I mean exactly that. What does worship mean? You will find that worship is respect that is paid to worth. If you go back and read the old marriage ceremonies, you will find that the bridegroom always said, "I with my body worship you." That is, he sees in her everything that is worthwhile. He must love her so much that he is willing to die for her.

Now the Bible is very expressive, and I do not know why we should be so reluctant to speak as plainly. If you turn back to the Song of Solomon, you will see the picture of the bridegroom and what he thinks of his bride: "Thou art all fair, my love; there is no spot in thee. . . . As the lily among thorns, so is my love among the daughters" (Song 4:7; 2:2). That is rather expressive, is it not? That is what the bridegroom says. Now hear the words of the bride: "My beloved is mine, and I am his: he feedeth among the lilies" (Song 2:16). You do not go any higher than that! In that moment of supreme and sweet ecstasy, either the wife will carry him to the skies or plunge him down to the depths of hell. Either the husband will place her on a pedestal and say, "I worship you because I find no spot in you," or else he will treat her with brutality. When the latter happens, he will kill her love, and she will hate him and become cold and frigid. In counseling we find that this is one reason that a great many marriages are breaking up.

Bacteriologist Rene Dubos of the Rockefeller Institute has made this statement, "Aimlessness and lack of fulfillment constitute the most common cause of organic and mental disease in the Western world." This is breaking up many a marriage. A wife becomes dissat-isfied and frustrated: she becomes nervous, neurotic, and nagging. And the husband settles down to a life of mediocrity: he becomes lonely and either develops into a henpecked Mr. Milquetoast or a domineering brute. You will find both in our society.

Now let me ask a question, and this is rather personal: Are you the kind of woman that a man would die for? I am going to be very frank. If you are just one of these little beetle-brains who is merely a sex kitten making eyes at every boy that comes along, although you may have a hairdo like a Navy balloon that is ready to make an ascension on the poop deck of a destroyer, you will never be the kind of woman that a man would die for. If you do not have beauty of character, if you do not have nobility of soul, you will be but a flame without heat, a rainbow without color, and a flower without perfume. The Word of God deals with the outward adorning—and do not misunderstand, the Bible does not militate against it. All of us ought to look the best we can—some of us have our problems, but we should do the best we can with what we have. God intends us to enhance the beauty He has given us. There is no reason for any woman not to dress in style. But God puts the emphasis, not on the outward adorning, but on the meek and quiet spirit, the inward adorning, which is with God of great price. "Whose adorning let it not be that outward adorning of plaiting the hair, and of wearing of gold, or of putting on of apparel; but let it be the hidden man of the heart, in that which is not corruptible, even the ornament of a meek and quiet spirit, which is in the sight of God of great price" (1 Pet. 3:3-4).

Now, young man, are you the kind of man that a woman would follow to the ends of the earth? You may look like a model for Hart, Schaffner and Marx but have no purpose, no ambition, no heart for serving God as a Christian, no capacity for great and deep things, no vision at all. If you are that kind, a woman will not follow you very far. She may go with you down to get the marriage license, but she also will be going down to get the divorce later on.

All across our west there are monuments erected to the pioneer wife and mother. I noticed one as I was traveling through Colorado. She is a fine-looking woman, crowned with a sunbonnet, the children about her holding on to her long, flowing dress. You know she did not go to the psychiatrist or the marriage counselor. Do you know why she never had to go to the preacher to talk about her marriage breaking up? Because one day a man came to her and said, "I am going west to build a career and home. Will you follow me?" She said, "I will." And she learned that this man would stand between her and danger; she had many experiences when he protected her from the menacing Indians of that day. She had no problems about whether he loved her or not. And he did not doubt her loyalty. They loved each other. These are the kind of people who built our country. It is the other element that is tearing it to pieces—my lovely country—how I hate to see it happening.

I know that someone is saying right now, "Preacher, I am not that kind of person. I'm no hero." Young man, God never said that every girl would fall in love with you. Ninety-nine women may pass you by and see in you only the boy next door who uses that greasy kid stuff. That's all. But let me say to you very seriously, one of these days there will come by a woman who will see in you the knight in shining armor. It is God who gives that highly charged chemistry between a certain man and a certain woman.

A young woman may be saying, "But I'm not beautiful of face or figure." May I say this to you, God never said that you would attract every male—only animals do that. Ninety-nine men will pass you by and see in you no more than what Kipling described as "a rag, a bone and a hank of hair." But one of these days there will come by a man who will love you if you are the right kind of person. You will become his inspiration. You may inspire him to greatness—to write a book, to compose a masterpiece of poetry or music, to paint a picture, or even to preach a sermon. If you are his inspiration, do not ignore him, do not run from him. God may have sent you together for that very purpose. There will come that one.

Perhaps you are thinking, "Preacher, you are in the realm of theory. What you are talking about is idealistic. It sounds good in a storybook, but it does not happen in life." You are wrong. It does happen.

I think of the story of Matthew Henry. I'm sitting right now in my office looking at a set of books called *Matthew Henry's Commentary*. If anyone ever wrote a musty commentary, Matthew Henry did. Although a great work, it is to me the most boring thing I have ever read. I never knew that fellow was romantic at any time in his life. But when he came to London as a young man, he met a very wealthy girl of the nobility. He fell in love with her, and she loved him. Finally she went to her father to tell him about it. The father, trying to discourage her, said, "Why, that young man has no background. You do not even know where he came from!" She answered, "You are right. I do not know where he came from, but I know where he is going, and I want to go with him." She went.

Nathaniel Hawthorne was merely a clerk that anybody would have passed by, working at the customs in New York City—until he was fired for inefficiency. He came home and sank into a chair, discouraged and defeated. His wife came behind him, placed before him pen and paper, and putting her arm about him, said, "Now, Nathaniel, you can do what you always wanted to do—you can write." He wrote The House of Seven Gables, The Scarlet Letter, and other enduring literature—because a wife was his inspiration. Theirs was an eternal love. "In one of her last letters the widow of Nathaniel Hawthorne penned this ineradicable hope, which became an anchor of comfort in her soul's sorrow: 'I have an eternity, thank God, in which to know him more and more, or I should die in despair' " (Walter A. Maier, For Better Not For Worse, p. 556).

You say I am talking about theory? I am talking about fact. Let us go back to the very beginning. Consider Adam and Eve. That was a romance! Listen to this: "So ought men to love their wives as their own bodies. He that loveth his wife loveth himself. [She is the other part of you. She's you.] For no man ever yet hated his own flesh; but nourisheth and cherisheth it, even as the Lord the church: for we are members of his body, of his flesh, and of his bones. For this cause shall a man leave his father and mother, and shall be joined unto his wife, and they two shall be one flesh" (Eph. 5:28–31).

Eve was created to be a helpmeet—a help that fit—for Adam. The language is tremendous. She was taken from his side, not molded from the ground as were the animals, but taken from a part of him so that he actually was incomplete until they were together. God fashioned her the loveliest thing in His creation, and He brought her to Adam. She was a helpmeet; she compensated for what he lacked, for he was not complete in himself. She was made for him, and they became one.

"And Adam said, This is now bone of my bones, and flesh of my flesh: she shall be called Woman, because she was taken out of Man. Therefore shall a man leave his father and his mother, and shall cleave unto his wife: and they shall be one flesh" (Gen. 2:23–24).

Let me move down in history. I want to mention a story that always thrilled me. It is the story of Abelard and Heloise. When John Lord wrote his *Great Women*, he used Heloise as the example of love, marital love. The story concerns a young ecclesiastic by the name of Abelard. He was a brilliant young teacher and preacher in what became the University of Paris. The canon there had a niece by the name of Heloise whom he sent to be under Abelard's instruction. She was a remarkable woman; he was a remarkable man. You know the story—they fell madly in love. But according to the awful practice of that day—and this day as well—the marriage of a priest was deemed a lasting disgrace. When John Lord wrote their story, he gave this instruction, which I would like to share with you. It is almost too beautiful to read in this day. It is like a dew-drenched breeze blowing from a flower-strewn mountain meadow over the slop bucket and pigsty of our contemporary literature. Here is what he wrote:

When Adam and Eve were expelled from Paradise, they yet found one flower, wherever they wandered, blooming in perpetual beauty. This flower represents a great certitude, without which few would be happy,—subtle, mysterious, inexplicable,—a great boon recognized alike by poets and moralists, Pagan and Christian; yea, identified not only with happiness, but human existence, and pertaining to the soul in its highest aspirations. Allied with the transient and the mortal, even with the weak and corrupt, it is yet immortal in its nature and lofty in its aims,—at once a passion, a sentiment, and an inspiration.

To attempt to describe woman without this element of our complex nature, which constitutes her peculiar fascination is like trying to act the tragedy of Hamlet without Hamlet himself,—an absurdity; a picture without a central figure, a novel without a heroine, a religion without a sacrifice. My subject is not without its difficulties. The passion or sentiment is degrading when perverted, it is exalting when pure. Yet it is not vice I would paint, but virtue; not weakness, but strength; not the transient, but the permanent; not the mortal, but the immortal,—all that is ennobling in the aspiring soul [John Lord, *Beacon Lights of History*, pp. 23-24].

Abelard and Heloise, having fallen in love, were not permitted by the church to marry. Therefore, they were married secretly by a friend of Abelard. He continued to teach. But the secret came out when a servant betrayed them, and she was forced into a nunnery. She was never permitted to visit him, and he was never permitted to visit her. Abelard was probably the boldest thinker whom the Middle Ages produced. At the beginning of the twelfth century, he began to preach and teach that the Word of God was man's authority, not the church. This man, a great man, became bitter and sarcastic in his teaching because of what had been denied him. When he was on his deathbed, for he died a great while before Heloise, being twenty years her senior, he asked that she be permitted to come to see him. The church did the cruelest thing of all—they would not allow her to come. Therefore he penned her a letter. To me it is the most pathetic thing I have ever read. He concludes it with this prayer:

> When it pleased Thee O Lord, and as it pleased Thee, Thou didst join us, and Thou didst separate us. Now what Thou hast so mercifully begun, mercifully complete; and after separating us in this world, join us together eternally in heaven.

It is my personal belief that in God's heaven they are together.

This brings us to a tremendous verse. Malachi has concluded the section on social sins which relate to the family and divorce. They were sins which were like a cancer gnawing at the vitals of the nation. And they will destroy any nation—ours will not be an exception, I am sure.

Ye have wearied the LORD with your words. Yet ye say, Wherein have we wearied him? When ye say, Every one that doeth evil is good in the sight of the LORD, and he delighteth in them; or, Where is the God of judgment? [Mal. 2:17].

"Ye have wearied the LORD with your words." I can't help but laugh at that. God says, "I'm so tired of those long, pious prayers that you say. And I am so tired of your testimonies. You really make Me weary." You remember that back in the first chapter they had said of their perfunctory service to God, "Behold, what a weariness is it." God says, "You don't know the half of it. You bore Me to tears by your hypocritical service."

"Yet ye say, Wherein have we wearied him?" We see again the feigned injured innocence of these people. They are offended that God would dare say this of them—they are entirely ignorant of their sins. They ask, "In what way have we wearied Him?"

Note that this is the fifth sarcastic question of the people to God's charge of their phony and pseudo worship. Contemptuously and impudently, they contradict God—"In what way have we wearied Him?"

Well, God has an answer for them. He lays it on the line and tells it to them like it is: "When ye say, Every one that doeth evil is good in the sight of the LORD, and he delighteth in them; or, Where is the God of judgment [justice]?" They are maligning the character of God.

This is a philosophy that arises rather frequently in the history of mankind. Man says, "Look, I see men who are big sinners and yet they are prosperous. They don't seem to have problems or trouble like I have—yet I am trying to serve the Lord. Why does God permit that sort of thing?"

The psalmist expresses this same complaint. He saw folk about him who were getting by with evil and not serving God at all. Yet they were the ones who seemed to prosper the most. He wrote: "But as for me, my feet were almost gone; my steps had well nigh slipped. For I was envious at the foolish, when I saw the prosperity of the wicked" (Ps. 73:2–3). As he looked around, he saw the rascals getting richer and richer while the poor got poorer and poorer. And the poor saints of God were the ones who were not prospering at all.

This was exactly the complaint of the people in Malachi's day. And that attitude produces very quickly a "new morality." When they feel that "every one that doeth evil is good in the sight of the LORD," they begin to call evil good and good evil. It pays to do evil.

We have much the same attitude in our day. Most people would say that crime does pay. People get by with as much as they possibly can. This applies to the big corporations as well as to the average man. The government spends our money without any kind of responsibility to the people. The lackadaisical attitude in Washington is one of the real problems in the world today. The politicians try to curry favor with the rich and please the powerful. The little man is stepped on, and nobody cares. Why doesn't God do something about it?

The psalmist got his answer to this problem because he went to God. "Until I went into the sanctuary of God; then understood I their end" (Ps. 73:17). You see, he had been looking at the immediate present. But how about the far-off future? What about their eternal state? From where you and I stand, their little day is ancient history, but way back then they made their decision for eternity. And for our generation time is slipping through the shuttle fast, let me tell you. So what about the godless today? Well, they can build a "new morality," they can accumulate as much money as they can, but those who do evil today will face the Judge tomorrow. They are going to answer to Him. We need to be very careful about sitting in judgment upon the apparent inaction of God in our contemporary society.

This reminds me of an incident when two of us seminary students were traveling together and picked up a hitchhiker who reeked of alcohol. He smelled like a still that had just come out of the Kentucky hills. He apologized for it and said that he knew he shouldn't drink. We witnessed to him of Christ, and my friend said something that was startling to me at that time, but I certainly concur with it now. He said to him, "We're not condemming you for getting drunk. You are a lost man on the way to hell; so you had better squeeze this life like an orange and get all you can of its juice while you're here. You won't have this liquor when you get over there. Go ahead and live it up. But you are moving into eternity. Did you ever stop to think about that?"

Any unsaved person who is familiar with the Word of God knows that he is a sinner and that there is a God of justice. But don't expect God to move in judgment immediately.

When I was a kid in southern Oklahoma, we used to swipe watermelons. I am honest with you when I say that every time I went into the watermelon patch to swipe a watermelon, I thought that there would be lightning out of heaven that would strike me dead. But I was going to steal those watermelons regardless! That is the willfulness of the human heart—even of a little boy.

However, the Lord doesn't operate quite like that, although He may do so. Because God does not always judge immediately, man interprets this to mean that God will not judge him at all. "Because sentence against evil work is not executed speedily, therefore the heart of the sons of men is fully set in them to do evil" (Eccl. 8:11). If a man gets by with it once, he will figure that he can just keep on getting but with it.

The people in Malachi's day asked, "Where is the God of justice?" Well, God will give them His answer in the following chapter.

CHAPTER 3

THEME: The prediction of the two messengers; the people rebuked for religious sins

Chapter 3 opens with God's answer to the question raised by the people of Israel at the end of the previous chapter.

> **Behold, I will send my messenger, and he shall prepare the way before me: and the Lord, whom ye seek, shall suddenly come to his temple, even the messenger of the covenant, whom ye delight in: behold, he shall come, saith the LORD of hosts [Mal. 3:1].**

Here in one verse we have two messengers. The first messenger who is to go before and to prepare the way is John the Baptist. The second is "the messenger of the covenant," the Lord Jesus Christ.

The prophecy concerning the first messenger is quoted in all four of the Gospels as applying to John the Baptist; there is no guesswork here. However, the messenger of the covenant is never quoted anywhere in the Gospels, and the reason is obvious. This messenger of the covenant is the Lord Jesus, but this passage hasn't anything to do with His first coming. This is His coming not in grace, not as a Redeemer, but as a Judge, as the One who will establish His Kingdom and put down the rebellion that is on this earth. You remember that on one occasion He even said to a man, ". . . who made me a judge or a divider over you?" (Luke 12:14). He hasn't come yet to judge. He came the first time to save. He came to bring grace, not government. He came as the One who is the Savior, not the Sovereign.

I would like to turn now to the Gospel passages which quote this verse in reference to John the Baptist. The first one is in Matthew 11:9–10: "but what went ye out for to see? A prophet? yea, I say unto you, and more than a prophet. For this is he, of whom it is written, Behold, I send my messenger before thy face, which shall prepare thy way before thee." Over in Mark's Gospel we find: "As it is written in the prophets, Behold, I send my messenger before thy face, which shall prepare thy way before thee" (Mark 1:2). Then in the Gospel of Luke we read, "This is he, of whom it is written, behold, I send my messenger before thy face, which shall prepare thy way before thee" (Luke 7:27). Finally, John 1:23 records, "He said, I am the voice of one crying in the wilderness, Make straight the way of the Lord, as said the prophet Esaias." This is a direct quote from Isaiah, but we can see that Malachi also had this to say about John the Baptist.

Therefore, this is God's answer to the people of Israel: God will send Him first as a Savior because He is gracious and He wants to save. But that doesn't end it all: He is coming again as the messenger of the covenant, that is, to execute justice and judgment on this earth.

If you could convince me that God does not intend to judge sin and that He intends to let sinners get by with their injustice today, then I say very frankly that I would turn my back on Him. But He's made it very clear that *He does intend to judge mankind.* My friend, if you will not have Him as your Savior, you're going to have Him as your judge whether you like it or not. He said, "For the Father judgeth no man, but hath committed all judgment unto the Son" (John 5:22). And in the Book of Revelation, we see a Great White Throne upon which He is seated. And those who are the lost—both rich and poor, high and low, great and small—are going to stand before it. It does not matter who you are, you are not going to get by with sin, my friend.

When it says "the messenger of the covenant," we need to understand which covenant is meant. A great many have thought that it is the New Covenant in the New Testament. Actually, this has no reference to the first coming of Christ but rather to the covenant which God has made with the people of Israel. This covenant is expressed in several places in the Scriptures. For instance, in Leviticus 26:9–13 we read: "For I will have respect unto you, and make you fruitful, and multiply you, and establish my covenant with you. And ye shall eat old store, and bring forth the old because of the new. And I will set my tabernacle among you: and my soul shall not abhor you. And I will walk among you, and will be your God, and ye shall be my people. I am the LORD your God, which brought you forth out of the land of Egypt, that ye should not be their bondmen; and I have broken the bands of your yoke, and made you go upright."

This is the covenant which God made with the children of Israel. You will find that He confirmed it in Deuteronomy, as the Book of Deuteronomy is a confirmation of the Mosaic Law and the Israelites' experience with it after forty years. Deuteronomy 4:23 says, "Take heed unto yourselves, lest ye forget the covenant of the LORD your God, which he made with you, and make you a graven image, or the likeness of any thing, which the LORD thy God hath forbidden thee." Of course, Israel had done the very thing which He had forbidden, turning even to the occult.

Therefore, Malachi tells us that the messenger of the covenant is coming someday to make good this covenant. God will dwell in their midst, and this is the reason we will also find in these first verses of Malachi 3 the cleansing and the purifying that will take place. God will not walk among them unless they are obedient unto Him, unless He has cleansed them and purified them. This is true, of course, of any Christian work today as well.

"The Lord, whom ye seek." This will be the Lord Jesus Christ, who is God manifest in the flesh.

"Shall suddenly come to his temple." This does not mean that He will soon come to His temple, but that when He comes it will be suddenly. A man once said to me, "You talk about the Rapture in which the Lord will take the church out of the world. Well, when that takes place and He removes the church and I see them leaving, then I'm going to accept Christ." But I said, "It will be too late then because the reason that He's taking the church out is that it is completed. So you would not be able then to be a part of the church. You could accept Christ and go through the Great Tribulation, but I think you're a fool to wait until then."

He is called the Lord, this is His temple, and He's the messenger of the covenant—so we know this is the Lord Jesus Christ. The One whom we know in the New Testament as the Lord Jesus Christ is the angel of the covenant in the Old Testament.

> **But who may abide the day of his coming? and who shall stand when he appeareth? for he is like a refiner's fire, and like fullers' soap [Mal. 3:2].**

We know that Malachi refers to the second coming of Christ because it is judgment that is in view here. Note the expression: "But who may abide the day of his coming?" This is the second coming of Christ.

"And who shall stand when he appeareth? for he is like a refiner's fire." In the refining process, the metal is put over red–hot fire, and as it begins to melt, the dross can be drawn off, and the metal is finally made pure.

"And like fullers' soap." He intends to purify, and He intends to clean. Purify and clean—there's not going to be any pollution when He establishes the Millennium on this earth.

> **And he shall sit as a refiner and purifier of silver: and he shall purify the sons of Levi, and purge them as gold and silver, that they may offer unto the LORD an offering in righteousness [Mal. 3:3].**

"And he shall sit as a refiner and purifier of silver: and he shall purify the sons of Levi." He is going to cleanse those who enter the Millennium.

"And purge them as gold and silver." There are two processes: cleansing and purifying. Cleansing is the use of soap as it is expressed here. And the fire is used for testing—this is another way which God has of purifying us and testing us.

> **Then shall the offering of Judah and Jerusalem be pleasant unto the LORD, as in the days of old, and as in former years [Mal. 3:4].**

"Then shall the offering of Judah and Jerusalem be pleasant unto the LORD." The Lord will take a great delight in their sacrifice because the ones who are offering it are now cleansed and purified. God is not interested in your going through rituals until your heart is right, until you have forsaken your sin and turned from it. You can get into sin, but if you stay in it, God is not accepting your religion at all.

"As in the days of old, and as in former years." In the time of Solomon, there was a period in which Israel served God in such a way that they witnessed to the entire world.

> **And I will come near to you to judgment; and I will be a swift witness against the sorcerers, and against the adulterers, and against false swearers, and against those that oppress the hireling in his wages, the widow, and the fatherless, and that turn aside the stranger from his right, and fear not me, saith the LORD of hosts [Mal. 3:5].**

"And I will come near to you to judgment; and I will be a swift witness against the sorcerers." Again, through these mixed marriages, through marrying heathen and pagan women who worshiped idols, their sorcery, the occult, and demon worship were brought in.

And in order to fill the great spiritual vacuum that is in our country, multitudes are turning to the occult today. This is the reason the movie *The Exorcist* was so popular. What a reflection this is on the church, which certainly has failed to fill that void.

"And against the adulterers." This is a reference to those who had made the mixed marriages by divorcing their wives and marrying these foreign heathen women.

"And against false swearers"—that is, liars.

"And against those that oppress the hireling in his wages, the widow, and the fatherless, and that turn aside the stranger from his right, and fear not me, saith the LORD of hosts." In other words, the people were not witnessing for God. The stranger in that day, to whom they should have witnessed, actually turned from God because of the way he was treated by God's people.

> **For I am the LORD, I change not; therefore ye sons of Jacob are not consumed [Mal. 3:6].**

God is a God of judgment, but He is also gracious. The reason that they had not been absolutely obliterated like the Edomites was because of His grace; it was because God is gracious. And He is still gracious because He never changes. Thank God for that. God today is still a God of judgment—that is a terror to the wicked. But He's also a God who never changes in reference to His grace—and that is a comfort to anyone who will accept the grace of God.

We come now to the sixth of these very smart-alecky retorts which these people give to God. There are eight of them in the book; we've seen five of them, and now we've come to the sixth. These people are, as it were, putting God on a quiz program. God makes a statement, and they ask Him to prove it. God brings eight incriminating accusations against the nation, and they counter by asking eight very impertinent and presumptuous questions. God answered them politely but emphatically. He is attempting to detour them from the destruction to which they are headed.

To interpret these questions it might be well to pause here again to consider the generation who asked them. After the people of Israel had been in captivity for seventy years, a remnant returned to the land. Reluctantly and halfheartedly, they set about restoring the city and rebuilding the temple. They had known the rigors and suffering of slavery. Like their fathers in the brickyards of Egypt, they had certainly been groaning. And even upon returning, they endured hardships, severe persecutions, and discouragements. Believe me, they thought that when they returned everything would be happy and nice and easy for them—but that was not the case. These were God's methods of discipline; it was a form of correction, but it did not have the desired effect. Discipline will either soften or harden you, and these people became hardened and embittered under the yoke which galled them. They became as hard as nails. They were like a prison inmate who has been released but not reformed. They had come out of slavery but apparently had not learned the lesson.

Actually, there is not much more that God could have done for them. Even God exhausted His infinite arsenal of correction. It was out of the soil of this generation that there grew up the poisonous plant of the Pharisees, the Sadducees, and the scribes who were in existence at the time when the Lord Jesus came four hundred years later. What was a pimple of rebellion against God in the time of Malachi, just a scratch on the surface of the nation, became at the time of the Lord Jesus an internal cancer.

God tried to stem the spread of the virus, to cauterize it, and He brought these eight charges against them. Their response reveals their attitude. They pled not guilty to every one of the charges, and they expressed surprise that God would even suspect them. They affected an injured innocence. They feigned hurt feelings. They assumed ignorance. They played the part of being highly offended, and with a wave of the hand, they dismissed the charges as unworthy of them.

This now is the sixth sarcastic question that the people give to God's penetrating charge. God is now going to call on the people to do something—

Even from the days of your fathers ye are gone away from mine ordinances, and have not kept them. Return unto me, and I will return unto you, saith the LORD of hosts. But ye said, Wherein shall we return? [Mal. 3:7].

Oh, what smart alecks they were! They say to God, "You say that we should return to You. We didn't know that we had gone away. We've been going up to the temple to all the services. We tithe to a certain extent. We're doing this, that, and the other thing, but how can we return when we haven't even left You?" They were actually so far gone that they did not realize their true condition.

I would say that this is pretty much the picture of a great many folk in the church today. Ritualism has been substituted for reality. Pageantry has been substituted for power. The aesthetic has been substituted for the spiritual, and form for feeling. Even in the orthodox, conservative, and evangelical circles, they know the vocabulary, but the power of God is gone. They are satisfied with a tasteless morality, they follow a few little shibboleths, and they feel that everything is all right.

But God says, "Return! You've departed from Me." What does He mean by returning to Him? He means to repent. To repent is to return to Him. God has said only to those who are His people, "Repent. Return to Me." You see, the unbeliever can't quite fulfill the song which says, "Lord, I'm coming home." The unbeliever hasn't even been home; he doesn't even have a home. The prodigal son had to *leave* a home before he could come back to his home. He was a son all the time. But he left home, and he had to repent and to change his mind. This is what repentance actually means.

We do not get the full meaning of repentance until we come to the New Testament. *Metanoia*, the Greek word, means "to change your mind." It means to be walking in one direction, realize you're going the wrong way, and turn right around and go the opposite way. The other day Mrs. McGee and I drove over to Glendale, which is a city right next to Pasadena here in Southern California. We asked for directions for getting to a certain place, and a girl gave us the wrong directions. She said, "Turn left," but when we turned left, we ran right up to the side of a mountain. I said to Mrs. McGee, "I think the girl told us wrong." So what did we do? We turned around. We had to return back to where we had turned off, and then we went the other direction and found that the other direction was the right direction. When I turned around, it was because I had found out I was wrong and I wanted to go the right way—that's repentance.

Now God speaks to His own about repentance. The interesting thing is that in the New Testament it is always believers to whom God says, "Repent." It is to those who are supposed to have been His children that He says, "Repent." In the Book of Revelation God had a message for each of the seven churches. To five of those churches God said, "Repent," but to the martyr church of Smyrna He didn't say that. They were dying for Him, and therefore He wouldn't say that. And to the church of Philadelphia, which was holding to the Word of God, He did not say, "Repent." But to all the rest of them, including the church at Laodicea, His message to the churches was to repent.

We have the notion today of telling the unsaved that they are to repent. Well, what are they to repent of? Do they need to change their direction? Yes, but repentance is not the message to be given to the unsaved. It is my feeling that the message of repentance is being given over the heads of believers to unbelievers, and it is falling on deaf ears, naturally. The people to whom it should be given are sitting right down in front. Believers are the ones to whom you should say, "Repent."

Somebody says, "Do you mean that the unsaved person who comes to Christ should not repent?" My friend, all the repentance that he is asked to do is in the word *believe.* Consider Paul's message to the Thessalonians. Paul had a very marvelous ministry there, and he said, "For they themselves shew of us what manner of entering in we had unto you, and how ye turned to God from idols to serve the living and true God" (1 Thess. 1:9). When Paul went into the city of Thessalonica, he did not preach to them against idolatry. It was running riot, but he didn't preach against it. He didn't preach against alcoholism or any of that type of thing. This is the reason that I don't follow the pattern of preaching against certain sins; only when the Word of God touches on these things do I touch on them. Our message to the lost world is what Paul gave to the Philippian jailer: ". . . Believe in the Lord Jesus Christ, and thou shalt be saved . . ." (Acts 16:31). In the word *believe* is all the repentance you need. When Paul went to Thessalonica and preached, did he preach repentance? No. He preached Christ. He said, "How ye turned to God *from* idols." The Thessalonians were going in one direction, and Paul said, "I want to tell you about Jesus Christ who died for your sins." And the Thessalonians turned to Christ. But when they turned to Him, they turned away from idols, and turning away is repentance—they turned around, you see— but it is in the word *believe.*

You must have something to turn *to,* my friend. You cannot just say to a man, "Repent." When I went down to an altar as a little boy, nobody counseled with me. I just wept—that was all. I wept because the boy next to me wept. His mother was a shoutin' Methodist, and she wept. She started all the weeping. The fellow across from me jumped up and said, "He's prayed through!" I don't know what he meant by that, but whatever it was I didn't do it. Nobody presented Christ to me. I was ready to repent because I wasn't the best boy in the world, although my mother thought so. I could weep for my sins, but I needed Christ. And when you turn to Christ, you'll turn from these things.

However, many of God's children, like the prodigal son, get into a far country, and He says, "Repent. Come home." That's the fellow who should come home. There are a lot of believers who need to come home. God is not talking about the unsaved fellow down the street. He's talking to you, and He says, "Come home." What are you doing in that liberal church? What are you doing committing adultery? God says, "Come on home. Turn around, and come on home." This is a message to believers. To these in Israel who were His children He said, "Return to me, and I will return unto you."

The prodigal son didn't get a whipping when he got home; he had gotten a whipping in the far country. If you think that pigpen was delightful, you are wrong. Any Christian who gets into sin will testify that it is not nearly as much fun as he thought it was going to be—many of us could say that. The important thing is to get out of the pigpen. My friend, there's not but one class of living creatures that like pigpens, and that is pigs. Sons just don't like pigpens, and they are going to get out.

The people of Malachi's day denied that they needed to return to God and repent. They acted as if they hadn't been anywhere. They say, "The temple is crowded. We're going through the ritual. What do You mean, 'Repent'? What do You mean, 'Return to You'? We're already here. We haven't gone anywhere!" But God says, "Yes, you have. You may be going through the ritual, but your heart is far from Me."

This is also true even in many conservative churches today. People go through the little ritual that we conservative folk have. We have a certain vocabulary. Folk know when to say, "Praise the Lord" and "Hallelujah," but their hearts are far from Him. He's asking us to repent, but it seems to be the most difficult thing to do, especially for Christians. I don't know why, because it should be easier for us than for any other people in the world.

I heard of a church where one of the officers got up and suggested to the board—who was finding fault with everything, including the pastor—that he felt the officers needed to repent. Do you know that they rebuffed that man and insulted him so that it apparently brought on his death? That was the way he was treated for even suggesting to a group of church officers that they needed to repent! Israel said,

"Wherein shall we return? How can we repent? We're beautiful people. We don't need to repent. That crowd outside needs to repent." There are a lot of folk in our churches today who think that everybody else needs to repent and that they don't. But we do need it, my friend. We need to return to God today.

When the people respond like this, believe me, God really opens up the wound here—and this will hurt. At this juncture some readers will want to tune me out because this is not going to be pleasant. I don't think that Malachi has been a very pleasant book, but I enjoy it because I think Malachi is talking right to me as well as to you or anybody else, and we need to be talked to like this.

My cancer doctor was a very wonderful doctor, but he treated me rougher than any doctor I have ever had. I tried to get him to give me an encouraging word every now and then. He wouldn't do it. I tried to get him to give me a prescription for easing pain, you know, but he wouldn't do it. He just laid it right on the line. I love the man, and I love him because of the fact that he told it like it was. When you've had cancer and you may still have it in your system, you really want to be told the truth. And in spiritual matters that have to do with my eternal soul, I want somebody to tell me the truth even if it hurts. God doesn't mind telling you the truth at all.

We come now to the seventh sarcastic remark that these people make. Eight times in this book these people will return to God a flippant answer. Eight times they will dismiss His charges like petulant children. Eight times they will evade the fact by affecting ignorance. Eight times they will avoid answering by pretending they are pious.

Will a man rob God? Yet ye have robbed me. But ye say, Wherein have we robbed thee? In tithes and offerings [Mal. 3:8].

Instead of pronouncing the benediction in many of our churches, the thing that probably should be said is this: "Stop thieves! You've been robbing God!" The congregation would be apt to say, "You don't mean us! We put a generous offering in the plate." Did you, my friend? Listen to this: "Will a man rob God? Yet ye have robbed me. But ye say,

Wherein have we robbed thee?" And God's answer is, "In tithes and offerings, you have robbed Me."

If you think that God is a Shylock of the sky who was trying to take something away from these people, you are wrong. What God was doing was actually blessing them and saying, "I'm going to let you have nine-tenths, and you return to Me one-tenth."

There are several rather important things that we do need to correct in our understanding at this point. To begin with, the people of Israel did not give just one tithe, as you would discover if you would examine the Scriptures carefully. I am indebted to Dr. Feinberg's excellent book on Malachi (pp. 125–126) in which he lists the tithes given by Israel:

The offerings in Israel were the first-fruits, not less than one-sixtieth of the corn, wine, and oil (Deuteronomy 18:4). There were several kinds of tithes: (1) the tenth of the remainder after the first-fruits were taken, this amount going to Levites for their livelihood (Leviticus 27:30–33); (2) the tenth paid by Levites to the priests (Numbers 18:26–28); (3) the second tenth paid by the congregation for the needs of the Levites and their own families at the tabernacle (Deuteronomy 12:18); and (4) another tithe every third year for the poor (Deuteronomy 14:28–29).

I would like to look more closely at this last Scripture because this is something that I feel should be observed today. I realize that our government has done much in an effort to help the poor—or maybe it's to help the bureaucrats. There is a real question as to who gets the money which is allocated for the poor. But my feeling is that the church ought to have more of an emphasis on helping the poor. Let's look at God's instructions to Israel: "At the end of three years thou shalt bring forth all the tithe of thine increase the same year, and shalt lay it up within thy gates: and the Levite, (because he hath no part nor inheritance with thee,) and the stranger, and the fatherless, and the widow, which are within thy gates, shall come, and shall eat and be satisfied; that the LORD thy God may bless thee in all the work of thine hand which thou doest" (Deut. 14:28-29). Therefore, every third year there was this extra tithe that was given for the poor. When you say that God required a tithe of Israel, what do you mean by it? We need to understand that there were several tithes which were given.

The second thing that we need to straighten out in our thinking is that we are living in the day of grace. The giving of believers today is on an altogether different basis than Israel's. We are to give, but on a different basis. The church is not under the tithe system as a legal system. That does not mean that some people couldn't give a tenth to the Lord—that may be the way the Lord would lead them to give. But let's notice the way the early church gave. When Paul wrote to the Corinthians, he used the Macedonians as an example: "How that in a great trial of affliction the abundance of their joy and their deep poverty abounded unto the riches of their liberality" (2 Cor. 8:2).

Though very poor, the Macedonians gave generously. "For to their power, I bear record, yea, and beyond their power they were willing of themselves" (2 Cor. 8:3).

They gave way beyond any tenth—the tithe didn't even enter into their thinking. They simply gave because of their love of the Lord. And Paul tells us another reason they gave—"Praying us with much entreaty that we would receive the gift, and take upon us the fellowship of the ministering to the saints" (2 Cor. 8:4).

You see, giving is fellowship. It is part of the fellowship and part of the worship of the church. "And this they did, not as we hoped, but first gave their own selves to the Lord, and unto us by the will of God" (2 Cor. 8:5).

This is the reason that from time to time I make it very clear that if you are an unsaved person, if you are not a Christian, we don't want you to give to our Bible-teaching radio ministry. To begin with, giving couldn't be a blessing to you, and I don't think that in the long run it would ever be a blessing to us. God asks His children to give. Have you ever noticed that the ark of the covenant was carried on the shoulders of the priests of Israel? The Lord could have called in somebody from the outside to carry it, or He could have had a cart to carry it because a cart carried some of the other things. But the ark of the covenant, which speaks of Christ, was carried on the shoulders of the priests. If we are going to carry forth His message about what He has done for us, it has to be carried upon the shoulders of those who are priests, those who are His. He's not asking you to give if you are not a Christian. "I speak not by commandment, but by occasion of the forwardness of others, and to prove the sincerity of your love" (2 Cor. 8:8).

Your giving proves your love for Christ. He doesn't ask you to give. The song which says, "I gave, I gave My life for thee, What hast thou given Me?" is as unscriptural as anything can be. He never asks you that question. He says, "If ye love me, keep my commandments" (John 14:15, italics mine). "For ye know the grace of our Lord Jesus Christ, that, though he was rich, yet for your sakes he became poor, that ye through his poverty might be rich" (2 Cor. 8:9).

Paul says that you should give hilariously, joyfully. When I was in Israel, I was shown several new government buildings, and one of them was their internal revenue service for the collection of taxes. My Jewish guide very wryly said, "We call that 'the new Wailing Wall.' " Let me remind you, when the offering is taken in our churches, it also is a wailing wall for some. People think, *Oh my, they are going to take an offering!* My friend, the offering ought to be a joyful part of the service. If you can't give joyfully, you ought not to be giving. It won't do you a bit of good, I can assure you of that.

In chapter 8 and on into chapter 9 of 2 Corinthians, Paul continues to discuss the basis upon which Christians are to give. I think that most Christians in this affluent society ought to be giving more than a tenth. Israel gave more than a tenth—there were four tithes.

When I was a pastor in Texas during the Depression, an elder in my church was the only one who was in a business that was really making money. I used to hunt on his ranch and also fish in the river which went right through his property. He and I were in his boat one day fishing when he said to me, "Preacher, why don't you preach more on the tithe?" I said, "Well, I don't believe in it." He did believe in the tithe and that was the way he gave. Every time he and I would get together he wanted to know why I didn't speak on the tithe. Finally, I went through 2 Corinthians 8 with him. Then I said, "There are a lot of Christians who ought to be giving more than a tenth. For example, I would say that you are probably making more money than any other individual in the church except the doctors." We had five doctors in the church, and they did well financially. But the point was that this man was really making money during the Depression. I told him, "I think that you ought to give more than a tenth." I looked him right straight in the eye when I said that, and he winced a little. He never again asked me to preach on the tithe because he was glad to give only his tenth. It eased his conscience to feel that that was all he ought to give.

A lot of folk ought to be giving more than a tenth, but when I say "ought to," that's me speaking. Jesus says, "Don't do it unless you are giving it because of love for Me and because you really want to get the Word out."

God says, "Will a man rob God?" What do you think? Again I say, instead of having the benediction at the end of the church service, they ought to let the people start to leave and then have somebody yell out, "Stop thieves!" There sure would be a whole lot of thieves who wouldn't want to be caught and would take out running. Why? Because they have robbed God. How did they rob God? Well, it all belongs to Him, but to Israel He said, "You keep nine-tenths, but I want you to give Me the other tenth to recognize Me."

It is amazing how some of the great businessmen of the past were Christians who gave to God and gave to God generously. The founder of the Hershey Chocolate Company was a Christian who was very regular in giving to the Lord. William Wrigley, the founder of the Wrigley Gum Company also gave generously to the Lord. I'm talking about the founders of these companies, not about the present generations. The J. C. Penney stores were started by a preacher's son whose father died when he was a boy. There were no arrangements made to care for his mother, except for people to say, "The Lord bless you." As a little boy, he had to go out and collect the clothes which his mother washed for a living, and he said, "When I grow up, I'm going to make money and see to it that no preacher's widow has to work like this." He made good, and he established villages where retired preachers and their wives can live. God has blessed these men in the past who have recognized Him. I believe that this is still true today, but, my friend, you will have to do it out of love—that is the only way He will accept it.

Ye are cursed with a curse: for ye have robbed me, even this whole nation [Mal. 3:9].

Under grace God wants you to give as you are able to give. For some people that would be less than the tithe, and for other people it would be more than the tithe. And I'm of the opinion that a great many in this affluent society ought to be giving more to God.

Here in Southern California there are headquarters or semi-headquarters of three of the major cults. One of the things that they do is to put their people back under the Mosaic Law and insist that they keep the law, including the tithes—that's part of the system. If you're going to belong to their group, you're going to give a tithe. Those three cults are very wealthy. We think that this little operation that we represent is great—we thank God for it—but we are actually a Mickey Mouse operation if you put us down by the side of these other organizations where millions of dollars are just rolling in. Even on the tithe, the old legal system, look at how much would come in. Doesn't that tell you that God's people who are under grace are surely not giving to the Lord's work as they should?

This is one of the reasons that we do not see the blessing that should attend God's work. Many churches have a minister who is teaching the Word of God, but they don't seem to be going anywhere. God makes it clear that our giving is something that He looks at. If a church or an individual is not giving, God has not promised to bless them at all. I believe that God is going to bless any person who is devoted to Him—but not necessarily with material blessings. Paul tells us in Ephesians that we are blessed with ". . . all spiritual blessings in heavenly places in Christ" (Eph. 1:3). Therefore God, in a very gracious manner, will bless those who are generous with Him. This is a great principle that runs through the entire Word of God. Many churches which were Bible churches have just dried up and died on the vine, and it can all be traced to the fact that the people were not giving as they should to God. If we open our heart to Him, He'll open

His heart to us. Not for *physical* blessings—God promised us *spiritual* blessings—"all spiritual blessings in heavenly places in Christ."

God made good His promises to His people. In the time of Hezekiah there was a period of revival. In 2 Chronicles 31:10 we read: "And Azariah the chief priest of the house of Zadok answered him, and said, Since the people began to bring the offerings into the house of the LORD we have had enough to eat, and have left plenty: for the LORD hath blessed his people; and that which is left is this great store."

In other words, the people were giving *more* than enough. At the time that Israel built the tabernacle, Moses asked for offerings, and he had to stop the people from giving because they were bringing too much! That is the only case on record that I have heard of people being stopped from giving—but they did it in that day.

> Bring ye all the tithes into the storehouse, that there may be meat in mine house, and prove me now herewith, saith the LORD of hosts, if I will not open you the windows of heaven, and pour you out a blessing, that there shall not be room enough to receive it [Mal. 3:10].

Again I would remind you that we are not under the tithe system today. There are many humble believers with very little income for whom a tenth would be too much to give. There are others whom God has blessed in such a wonderful way that they could easily give even as much as the government will allow for deductions. There are those who have an income such that they could give that to the Lord, but we find very few who are giving like that. The tithe is certainly a yardstick by which you could measure yourself, but I don't think that it is legal or binding at all.

"Bring ye all the tithes into the storehouse." There are many churches and some denominations which have said that the storehouse is the local church or the denomination. Frankly, just as the tithe is not for the church today, neither is the storehouse. The storehouse was a part of the temple. There were many buildings around the temple which were storerooms. When people brought their tithe, it was stored away in these storerooms. When Nehemiah came back to Jerusalem (sometime before the time of Malachi), he found Tobiah, the enemy of God, living in one of the storerooms that had been cleaned out. It had been cleaned out because the people were not giving generously, and they had made an apartment out of it for Tobiah! But Nehemiah cleaned up the place. He took Tobiah's things and pitched them out the window and told him to get out of town. Then the people began to bring their offerings to fill up the storeroom again (see Neh. 13:4–9).

There is no such thing today as that which is called "storehouse giving." That's not quite the way we give, because Israel's giving was in the form of produce. In fact, if you will notice the law concerning the offerings, God gave a certain part of the animal to the priests, and He always said that they were to eat it right there. They didn't have any refrigerators, any kind of icebox, in which to freeze the meat. In that warm climate the meat would have gone bad in a hurry, and so God told them to eat it right there. But the other produce was stored until it was needed.

> **And I will rebuke the devourer for your sakes, and he shall not destroy the fruits of your ground; neither shall your vine cast her fruit before the time in the field, saith the LORD of hosts [Mal. 3:11].**

When they were generous with God, He said, "I'll open up the heavens and pour you out a blessing, and I'll rebuke the devourer." "The devourer" evidently means the locust. The locust had a ravenous and insatiable appetite. He was a regular gourmet on green salad—so he just took all the green stuff that was ahead of him. Many of the plagues came to Israel through the locust, but now God says, "I will rebuke the devourer for your sakes."

Even today judgment comes from God upon a nation when they reject Him. I think that this explains the fact that we are having so many shortages—not only an energy shortage but shortages in many areas. For years the shelves of our supermarkets were groaning because they were so full. My supermarket still does pretty well, but there are some things that are absent. You cannot always get the cut of meat that you would like to have. Even if they have it, you can't pay for it unless you mortgage your home! No one seems to be interpreting these things as a judgment or a warning from God. I think it is a warning of that which is to come in the future; in other words, I don't think we've seen anything yet.

"And he shall not destroy the fruits of your ground; neither shall your vine cast her fruit before the time in the field, saith the LORD of hosts." In other words, their vineyards were to produce abundantly.

> **And all nations shall call you blessed: for ye shall be a delightsome land, saith the LORD of hosts [Mal. 3:12].**

When Israel was right with God, they became a blessing to the other nations of the world. Honesty with God—and you cannot have holiness without honesty—was the thing that made them a blessing to all nations. In Zechariah 8:13 we read: "And it shall come to pass, that as ye were a curse among the heathen, O house of Judah, and house of Israel; so will I save you, and ye shall be a blessing: fear not, but let your hands be strong."

This looks forward to a future day, but God said at that time that He would make them a blessing to the nations. When Israel is serving God, it becomes a blessing to the other nations.

In verse 13 we come to the eighth and last sarcastic remark which the people of Israel make to God in response to His statements.

> **Your words have been stout against me, saith the LORD. Yet ye say, What have we spoken so much against thee? [Mal. 3:13].**

The people respond, "We don't recall that we have said anything against You!" In each of His responses God puts it right on the line—

> **Ye have said, It is vain to serve God: and what profit is it that we have kept his ordinance, and that we have walked mournfully before the LORD of hosts? [Mal. 3:14].**

Israel says, "What good is it for us to serve God? It is an empty thing." For them it was an empty thing because their hearts were not in it. And since their hearts were not in it, God had not blessed them. So they blamed God for the situation. They said, "It's not worthwhile to serve God." Well, the way they were doing it, it wasn't worthwhile.

I want to make a very strong statement right now. There are some people who attend church who, very frankly, I think would do better if they would just take a drive on Sundays. Their hearts are not in it. They go to church to criticize. As someone has said, "Some people go to eye the clothes and others to close their eyes." Some will go to church because it's a nice place to get a nap. If your heart is not in it, my friend, if you don't love God, if you don't want to praise Him and serve Him and worship Him, it is of no value.

Today our worship is on a very marvelous, wonderful plane. This is what the Lord Jesus said to the woman at the well: ". . . Woman, believe me, the hour cometh, when ye shall neither in this mountain, nor yet at Jerusalem, worship the Father. Ye worship ye know not what: we know what we worship: for salvation is of the Jews. But the hour cometh, and now is, when the true worshippers shall worship the Father in spirit and in truth: for the Father seeketh such to worship him. God is a spirit: and they that worship him must worship him in spirit and in truth" (John 4:21-24).

The Lord Jesus told this woman that the hour was coming when true worshipers would not worship God in that mountain; but believe me, they are still offering bloody sacrifices at that mountain. He said, "Nor yet at Jerusalem"— Jerusalem is not a place to worship God. Every form of so-called Christianity is found there, and most of it is as far from the message of the Lord Jesus and the early apostles as anything possibly could be. The Lord Jesus went on to say that true worshipers are going to worship God in spirit and in truth. They are going to love the Word of God. They'll want to serve Him. They'll want to obey Him. They'll want to worship and to praise Him.

A man said to me one time, "Well, McGee, I guess you think that I'm going to hell because I play golf on Sunday." I said, "No. You're not going to hell because you play golf on Sunday. You're going to hell because you've rejected the Lord Jesus Christ. Golf hasn't anything to do with it. I know a lot of church members who I wish would go play golf on Sunday to get them out of the church because they are trouble-makers. They are not worshiping God in spirit and in truth." My friend, all of this outward religion is not good. The crucial thing is the condition of your heart and your relationship to Jesus Christ.

It was vain and empty for the people in Malachi's day to worship God, but the problem wasn't with Him—the problem was with them. I went to see a man in the hospital many years ago. Outside the door of his room, his wife told me that the doctors said that he was dying. I went in to see him, to have prayer with him, and to say a word, not only of comfort but that his wife might have the assurance of his salva-tion. He said to me, "Dr. McGee, I'm about to freeze to death. Would you get that blanket over there and put it on me?" And I did. That room was hot—oh, it was hot—but that man thought he was freezing to death. He blamed it on the room and said, "They never keep these rooms warm." But the room was overheated. There are a great many people who say that the church they attend is cold. Are you sure that the church is cold, or is it maybe you who are cold? It might be well to check up, because the problem here was with the people—it was not with God at all.

I would like to look at a good definition of real worship which is given to us in the Scriptures in Isaiah 58: "Wherefore have we fasted, say they, and thou seest not? wherefore have we afflicted our soul, and thou takest no knowledge? Behold, in the day of your fast ye find plea-sure, and exact all your labours" (Isa. 58:3).

You see, they had the same problem way back in Isaiah's day that they had in Malachi's day. They fasted and they afflicted their souls, and God didn't do anything about it. "Behold, ye fast for strife and debate, and to smite with the fist of wickedness: ye shall not fast as ye do this day, to make your voice to be heard on high" (Isa. 58:4).

God says, "I don't care about your fasting, your going through all of that ritual, and your wanting to debate religion." They just wanted to have a religious argument. Quite frequently there comes to my desk a very fat letter from someone who wants to enter into a controversy with me or to straighten me out on some doctrinal point. Generally there are fifteen to twenty pages, sometimes closely typewritten or written in such a way that I couldn't even read it if I wanted to. I never read those letters. I'm sorry—maybe I'm missing something—but I just put them into the wastebasket. We won't get anywhere by arguing, my friend. You can differ with my interpretation if you want to. But if you believe that the Bible is the Word of God as I do, why don't you just pray for me if you think my interpretation is wrong. And my interpretation could be wrong, by the way—you ought to test it.

Now here is our definition of real worship: "Is not this the fast that I have chosen? to loose the bands of wickedness, to undo the heavy burdens, and to let the oppressed go free, and that ye break every yoke? Is it not to deal thy bread to the hungry, and that thou bring the poor that are cast out to thy house? when thou seest the naked, that thou cover him; and that thou hide not thyself from thine own flesh? Then shall thy light break forth as the morning, and thine health shall spring forth speedily: and thy righteousness shall go before thee; the glory of the LORD shall be thy rereward" (Isa. 58:6–8).

What Isaiah is saying is that when you come in to worship God, make sure you have a life to back it up. This is very important. God wants a life that will back up what you have to say. Here we have an Old Testament definition of real worship. The ritual itself has no value unless the heart is right before God. This is something that we need to remember and keep before us.

And now we call the proud happy; yea, they that work wickedness are set up; yea, they that tempt God are even delivered [Mal. 3:15].

It looked as if they could tempt God and get by with it, but as Habakkuk had found out in his day, God was moving in the life of the nation and was going to judge them. I am of the opinion that if we could see behind the scenes today and see the wheels of God that are moving, we would cry out to God to have mercy. He is moving, but we don't seem to recognize it.

Then they that feared the LORD spake often one to another: and the LORD hearkened, and heard it, and a book

of remembrance was written before him for them that feared the LORD, and that thought upon his name [Mal. 3:16].

"Then they that feared the LORD spake often one to another." In other words, there was a little remnant who loved God and met together, and they feared the Lord. They spoke to one another—they were having fellowship.

"And the LORD hearkened, and heard it, and a book of remembrance was written before him for them that feared the LORD, and that thought upon his name." Running all through the Scripture there is this idea that God keeps books. I do not think there is an actual book up there in which He is writing. God never forgets, and He doesn't need that book, and He doesn't even need a computer.

This matter of the book that was written is also mentioned in the Book of Revelation, and in chapter 3 we find the suggestion that He is apt to erase a name: "Thou hast a few names even in Sardis which have not defiled their garments; and they shall walk with me in white: for they are worthy. He that overcometh, the same shall be clothed in white raiment; and I will not blot out his name out of the book of life, but I will confess his name before my Father, and before his angels" (Rev. 3:4–5).

This is about as strong a language as you can get, and it is, very frankly, one of the most difficult passages in the Book of Revelation to understand. I do not think that God has a set of books that He is keeping in heaven. But the only way that you and I can understand this is through this figure of speech that He uses. I can understand it when He says that He puts down in the Book of Life the names of those who are saved. I can understand that He puts down in a book those who will receive a reward or some recognition. This makes it clear to me. But I don't believe that God has a literal book up there—although He may have. We are also told in the last part of the Book of Revelation that when the lost are brought before the Great White Throne, the books will be opened, and there are several of them. There is also the book of those who are saved (see Rev. 20).

I would like to illustrate it in this way: To me it is more or less like the report card I used to get in school. You get a report card if you are a student; all you have to do to get a report card is to enroll. You get into the Lamb's Book of Life by accepting Christ as your Savior, and that will never be removed. You have a report card; you are in the Lamb's Book of Life; you're enrolled. *Now* you are going to start making grades. *Now* He's going to put down how you are doing with your Bible study. What grade is He giving you on that? Are you making A's these days? Or are you failing the course? How is your life for Him? How is your service for Him? He takes note of all these things, and they are recorded.

Therefore I believe that when He says to the church of Sardis that names are removed from the Book of Life, that names are blotted out, it has to do with service because that is what He is talking about there. It has to do with the *service* that they render. There will be many of us who get a report card, but some are going to be a failure in the Christian life. Paul said in his Epistle to the Corinthians that our works are to be tested by fire (see 1 Cor. 3:11–15). If a man's work is all hay and stubble and it is all consumed by fire, will he be saved? Paul says, "Yes. He'll be saved, but so as by fire." There are going to be a lot of people in heaven who will smell like they were bought at a fire sale— and they were—a brand plucked from the burning, if you please. They did nothing, and nothing was put on the report card.

"A book of remembrance was written before him for them that feared the LORD, and that thought upon his name." God simply doesn't need a book to remember things because He is the One who really has a computer mind—it's all there. The record is of their works, their service, their love for Him—those are the things that are recorded. Salvation is free. It is by faith, never by works. After you have been saved, that is when your works really begin to count, and they become all-important. This book of remembrance is a very beautiful thing.

We find God's "book" mentioned elsewhere in the Old Testament. In Psalm 56:8 we read, "Thou tellest my wanderings: put thou my tears into thy bottle: are they not in thy book?" The psalmist says, "Thou tellest my wanderings." The Lord knows exactly where you've been all the time. Maybe your neighbors, your fellow church members, and your pastor don't know—but God knows. The darkness is light to Him. He knows where you've been and He knows what you've done. "Put thou my tears into thy bottle"—I think that is a very lovely thing. My friend, that godly mother who is weeping because of a wayward child, God has put those tears into a bottle. Can you imagine that? How wonderful it is that He has taken note of them! The man who has served God but has been disappointed by how his brethren have treated him and has wept tears over it—to him God says, "I've put those tears in a bottle." Finally, the psalmist says, "Are they not in thy book?" There is a book that records our lives, my friend. I have always thought that it is probably going to be sort of like a movie that He will run through for us. You will see your life from birth to death, and it will all be there. It won't be what the preacher said about you at your funeral, about how wonderful you were and what a great church member you were. God is going to run it just like it was. I don't want to see mine. But I guess I'll have to take a look at it someday.

> **And they shall be mine, saith the LORD of hosts, in that day when I make up my jewels; and I will spare them, as a man spareth his own son that serveth him [Mal. 3:17].**

Isn't this a lovely way to express it? God is going to make up His jewels, and the church is going to be there. The church is the pearl of great price. Israel never valued pearls very much; Gentiles always have. And so the pearl of great price is His church purchased with His own precious blood. God is going to make up His jewels, and there will be many of them.

"And I will spare them, as a man spareth his own son that serveth him." This speaks of the remnant of believers that there will be during this time.

> **Then shall ye return, and discern between the righteous and the wicked, between him that serveth God and him that serveth him not [Mal. 3:18].**

We are living in a day like the day in which Malachi lived and like it will be at the end of the age. You really won't be able to tell the righteous from the unrighteous. However, in the day which God has appointed, the day of His judgment when He comes again, it will be evident who are the true believers and who are the make–believers.

CHAPTER 4

THEME: *The prediction of the Day of the Lord and of the Sun of Righteousness*

In the Hebrew Bible there is no fourth chapter of the Book of Malachi; it is just the end of the third chapter. However, in the English translation, these six brief verses are made a separate chapter. In chapter 4 we have the prediction of the Day of the Lord and of the Sun of Righteousness who ushers it in. The first verse is a vivid description of the Great Tribulation period—

> For, behold, the day cometh, that shall burn as an oven; and all the proud yea, and all that do wickedly, shall be stubble: and the day that cometh shall burn them up, saith the LORD of hosts, that it shall leave them neither root nor branch [Mal. 4:1].

"For, behold, the day cometh"—this is the Day of the Lord.

"That shall burn as an oven; and all the proud, yea, and all that do wickedly, shall be stubble." In other words, they shall be consumed. In the Book of Revelation we read that at one fatal swoop one-fourth of the population of the world will be wiped out (see Rev. 6:8).

"And the day that cometh shall burn them up, saith the LORD of hosts, that it shall leave them neither root nor branch." This hasn't anything in the world to do with the doctrine that death ends all for the unsaved, that death for the unsaved is annihilation. The Bible doesn't teach that. The Bible teaches that the body goes into the grave whether a person is lost or saved. Your soul and spirit go into eternity, my friend—either to heaven or to hell. This verse teaches that the unsaved are to be judged in the Great Tribulation period and removed from the earth's scene.

> **But unto you that fear my name shall the Sun of righ-
> teousness arise with healing in his wings; and ye shall
> go forth, and grow up as calves of the stall [Mal. 4:2].**

The Sun of Righteousness in the Old Testament is the same person
who is the Bright and Morning Star in the New Testament. However,
Christ is never called the Sun of Righteousness in the New Testament,
and He's never called the Bright and Morning Star in the Old Testament. We will look at this verse more closely in a moment and see the
reason for this.

> **And ye shall tread down the wicked; for they shall be
> ashes under the soles of your feet in the day that I shall
> do this, saith the LORD of hosts [Mal. 4:3].**

When He comes to this earth to establish His Kingdom, the wicked
will be put down. He will break them into pieces like a potter's vessel.
That is the language of Scripture, and it is just too bad if you don't
like it.

> **Remember ye the law of Moses my servant, which I
> commanded unto him in Horeb for all Israel, with the
> statutes and judgments [Mal. 4:4].**

Following this prophecy by Malachi, Israel is going to move into a
period in which heaven goes off the air. God will not be broadcasting.
There will appear another Zechariah [Zecharias] four hundred years
later. He will be serving in the temple when the angel Gabriel will
appear to him and announce the birth of John the Baptist (see Luke
1:5–25). The silence of four hundred years will then be broken. In the
meantime, Israel is to remember the Law of Moses. It will be their life;
it will be God's Word for them. They were under the Mosaic system.

> **Behold, I will send you Elijah the prophet before the
> coming of the great and dreadful day of the LORD [Mal.
> 4:5].**

Revelation speaks of two witnesses who are to appear in the last days (see Rev. 11:3–12). I do not know who the second witness will be, but I am almost sure that one of them will be Elijah. At the Passover Feast, in the Orthodox Jew's home, a chair is put at the table in which no one sits. It is for Elijah who shall come. When John the Baptist appeared the Jews thought he was Elijah, but John the Baptist was not Elijah in any sense of the word. The Scriptures do say that he could have been, but he wasn't—and that's the important thing. If Christ had established His Kingdom, then John would have been Elijah. How could that be? I do not know because it didn't happen that way. That's an "iffy" question for which we cannot really have an answer.

"Behold, I will send you Elijah the prophet before the coming of the great and dreadful day of the LORD." John the Baptist was not the fulfillment of this prophecy because he was announcing the Messiah, the Savior of the world. John said, ". . . Behold the Lamb of God, which taketh away the sin of the world" (John 1:29). That is a little different from announcing the great and terrible Day of the Lord that is coming.

> **And he shall turn the heart of the fathers to the children, and the heart of the children to their fathers, lest I come and smite the earth with a curse [Mal. 4:6].**

The last word of the Old Testament is curse. The curse came when Adam and Eve were in the Garden of Eden and disobeyed God. At that time God said that the ground would be cursed and that the curse would rest upon them. The curse was sin, and it will not be removed until the Lord comes to this earth the second time. It is still in the human family today. All you have to do is to look about you to see that. If you are living in a place where you do not have snails, termites, or some other kind of blight eating away at whatever you are trying to raise—whether it is vegetables or flowers or trees—then you must have moved into the Millennium, my friend. And if you are living in a community where there is no sin, I'd have to say that you've already moved into the Millennium. But I'm of the opinion that, as we look about us today, we can recognize that the curse of sin is upon the human race and upon this earth.

This is a very doleful way to end the Old Testament, but it has been a book of expectations. Therefore, I think that the emphasis should be on verse 2 of this chapter: "But unto you that fear my name shall the Sun of righteousness arise with healing in his wings; and ye shall go forth, and grow up as calves of the stall." The Old Testament does not close with only a curse. It closes with a great hope that, although the sun has gone down and it is very dark, there is coming a new day. We are living in the night of sin, and the world is dark. It seems that we are at the darkest moment today. But there is coming a day when the Sun of Righteousness will rise and spiritual light will break upon this little planet.

That Sun of Righteousness is none other than the Lord Jesus Christ. I want to call your attention to something that is very remarkable and very important. In the Old Testament Christ is presented as the Sun of Righteousness. In the New Testament He's presented in a different way altogether. There He is presented to us as the Bright and Morning Star. Listen to Him as He speaks in Revelation 22:16, and this concludes Revelation: "I Jesus have sent mine angel to testify unto these things in the churches. I am the root and the offspring of David, and the bright and morning star." "The root and the offspring of David" means that He is the King who will reign on this earth, but He is also something else—"the bright and morning star," which is something new, by the way.

It is interesting that man's attention has always been drawn to the heavens. Astronomy is the oldest science known to man, but like many other sciences, it had its origin in the occult and superstition, in the mythological and the mystical. Astronomy as we know it actually had its origin in astrology, that which is filled with superstition. You might say, "That was way back yonder in the Dark Ages when men were very superstitious, but today we've improved." Have we improved? Right now there are probably more people in this country who are interested in the horoscope and the star under which they were born than are interested in the Bible, the Word of God, or anything else, for that matter. To those who are playing with the zodiac and its signs, may I say to you that it is something which borders on the occult. We're seeing today the worship of Satan as we've never seen it before. It is quite interesting that research shows that some years ago only 3 percent of those interviewed believed in a personal devil. More recently the percentage had jumped to 37–48 percent who believe and are convinced that there is a devil. Apparently, some who are not convinced that there is a God to whom they are responsible, do believe in the Devil.

The heavenly bodies are being observed by men today. At first they were observed with the naked eye because of curiosity about the beauty of the heavens. Then the mechanical eye came into existence, and now scientists are making a greater study of the heavens than they have ever made before.

Scripture does turn man's attention repeatedly to the heavens. Psalm 8 reads: "When I consider thy heavens, the work of thy fingers, the moon and the stars, which thou hast ordained; What is man, that thou art mindful of him? and the son of man, that thou visitest him?" (Ps. 8:3–4).

The answer to that question is that man happens to be the astronomer. He's the one who can view all of this and can give praise and glory to God. "The heavens declare the glory of God; and the firmament sheweth his handiwork" (Ps. 19:1). God said to Abraham, ". . . Look now toward heaven, and tell the stars, if thou be able to number them . . ." (Gen. 15:5).

The Old Testament closes here in Malachi with God directing man to look toward the heavens, and it is well that man looks up. Malachi closes with a thud: "Lest I come and smite the earth with a curse," and the curtain comes down before the human story is over. Darkness closes in on man, but the play is not over. There are the good guys and the bad guys, and the good guys haven't won yet. God says, "Look up at the heavens. Don't miss it." It is important that you see, my friend. He says, "But unto you that fear my name shall the Sun of righteousness arise with healing in his wings; and ye shall go forth, and grow up as calves of the stall." This is a promise of a sunrise. There is a song that says that the world is waiting for a sunrise—and I believe it is—but the church is waiting for something else. Kipling wrote a poem that has been made into a song which says in part, "An' the dawn comes up like thunder outer China 'crost the Bay!" When Christ the

Sun of Righteousness comes, that's the way He's going to come: out of the east He'll come up like thunder to put down all unrighteousness.

The Old Testament is expectation. In one sense it is the most disappointing book in the world if it stands by itself. But it points to the heavens, and it speaks of the Lord Jesus Christ, the Sun of Righteousness. This is a fitting figure for Him because He comes to usher in a new day and to end the night of man's sin. The Day of the Lord is coming, and His Kingdom will be established upon the earth. God is called a sun throughout the Old Testament. Listen to Psalm 84:11: "For the LORD God is a sun and shield: the LORD will give grace and glory: no good thing will he withhold from them that walk uprightly."

Then in Isaiah 60:19 we read: "The sun shall be no more thy light by day; neither for brightness shall the moon give light unto thee: but the LORD shall be unto thee an everlasting light, and thy God thy glory."

What a picture we have of Him in the Old Testament!

On the other hand, the New Testament is realization, and it closes with a little different hope. Let me repeat this marvelous verse: "I Jesus have sent mine angel to testify unto you these things in the churches. I am the root and the offspring of David, and the bright and morning star" (Rev. 22:16).

Not only is He the Sun of Righteousness, but He is also the Bright and Morning Star. It is quite interesting that the New Testament does not open with the Sun of Righteousness. The first public announcement was made privately to Zacharias. Then there was a promise of the coming of a forerunner, John the Baptist. The forerunner of whom? Of the Messiah who was coming, who was to be born of Mary. Wise men came to Jerusalem seeking what? They said, ". . . Where is he that is born King of the Jews? for we have seen his star in the ~ast, and are come to worship him" (Matt. 2:2, italics mine). By the way, that is not an eastern star. If they had seen an eastern star, they would have ended up in China. The wise men in the east saw the star, the star was in the west, and they came that direction. Isn't it interesting that the sun comes up from the east, but this star was in the west?

How did the wise men associate the coming of Christ with a star? Way back in the Book of Numbers, the heathen prophet Balaam, in the east in Moab, made this prophecy: "I shall see him, but not now: I shall behold him, but not nigh: there shall come a Star out of Jacob, and a Sceptre shall rise out of Israel, and shall smite the corners of Moab, and destroy all the children of Sheth" (Num. 24:17).

Always the star is separated from the sceptre. The star is separated from the sun. The star is the sign of the coming of Christ to take His church out of the world, and the sun is the sign of His second coming to the earth to establish His Kingdom. The Jewish apostles were told at the time of the Ascension, ". . . this same Jesus, which is taken up from you into heaven, shall so come in like manner as ye have seen him go into heaven" (Acts 1:11), and Zechariah tells us that His feet shall touch the Mount of Olives (see Zech. 14:4). The star, therefore, is the sign of His first coming to take His church out of the world, but He doesn't come to the earth. When He came before, the entire mission of Christ was wrapped up in a star and not as the Sun of Righteousness. The emphasis is not on His birth but rather on His death. It is interesting that He never asked anybody to remember His birth, but He did say to remember His death. When He established the Lord's Supper, over that Passover Feast, He took the dying embers of a fading feast, and He said, ". . . this do in remembrance of me" (Luke 22:19). The death of Christ as well as His birth is in that star. The star speaks not only of where He was born but also of why He died. The star tells out who He is, why He came. He said, ". . . Lo, I come (in the volume of the book it is written of me,) . . ." (Heb. 10:7). The star points to a manger, but it also points to a cross. It speaks of the fact that He came to bear my sins and yours upon the Cross.

A little boy was walking down the street with his father during World War II. He noticed that there were blue stars in many windows, but every now and then there would be a gold star in a window, which meant that someone had given a son to die for this country. It was in the early evening, and as they came to a vacant lot, the evening star was just appearing above the horizon. The little fellow said to his dad, "Look, Dad! God gave His Son!" Yes, God gave His Son, and the star speaks of that. The little fellow was right, by the way.

Certainly, in two world wars nothing was won—or in any war which we have fought since then. We thought we were going to make the world safe for democracy. Every president from Woodrow Wilson down to the present time has thought that he was going to bring peace into the world and make the world unsafe for dictators. Yet today over half the world is under dictators. We won the wars all right, but we sure lost the victory. In the war against sin the Lord Jesus died to bring men life, to free men from sin, and to bring victory over the grave and death. "O death, where is thy sting? O grave, where is thy victory?" (1 Cor. 15:55).

The future is not in the stars, my friend. In *Julius Caesar* Shakespeare has Cassius say to Brutus: "The fault, dear Brutus, is not in our stars, but in ourselves, that we are underlings" [act 1, scene 2].

Your future is not in stars out there and neither is your present. If you want help for the present, you need to live victoriously for Jesus Christ who said, "These things I have spoken unto you, that in me ye might have peace. In the world ye shall have tribulation: but be of good cheer; I have overcome the world" (John 16:33). Are you defeated and discouraged? There's no help in the stars for you, my friend! You're nothing in the world but a pagan and a heathen if you believe that. Look to Jesus. It's not some magic formula; it's not Lady Luck; it's not chance; it's not fatalism; it's not superstition. If you are defeated by life, if you are overcome by some habit—drink, dishonesty, temper, sex, or materialism—if you are cold and indifferent to spiritual things, may I say to you, He is the answer for you.

> Somewhere beyond the stars
> Is a Love that is better than Fate,
> And when night unlocks her bars,
> I shall see Him, and I shall wait.
>   —Author unknown

If you have no hope for the future, you can look back to a historic event that took place over nineteen hundred years ago when Christ died on the Cross for you and for me who are sinners. And you can trust Him as your Savior. Then you can turn your face to the sunrise because the Bright and Morning Star is going to appear one of these days.

Is there hope for the future? Oh, my friend, the bright and morning star appears right before the sun comes up. In my bedroom, I have four windows from which I can look out and see the sun come up. In the winter the sun comes up on the extreme right; in the summer it comes up on the extreme left. I watch the sun as it marches back and forth from one window to another. Last March and April I was watching as the bright and morning star appeared nearly an hour before the sun came up. The bright and morning star appears first, then the sun comes up. So we are waiting for the Bright and Morning Star to appear. Christ is the Bright and Morning Star for the church today—that is important to see. Peter speaks of Him in that way: "We have also a more sure word of prophecy; whereunto ye do well that ye take heed, as unto a light that shineth in a dark place, until the day dawn, and the day star arise in your hearts" (2 Pet. 1:19).

The day star speaks of the rapture of the church when He will take the church out of the world. The Rapture could take place at any moment in time, for there are no signs for it at all. John Wesley put it like this: "He will appear as the day-spring from on high, before the morning light. Oh, do not set us a time—expect Him every hour! Now He is nigh, even at the doors!" Job said that ". . . the morning stars sang together, and all the sons of God shouted for joy" (Job 38:7), but then sin entered God's universe. But the day is coming when that Day Star shall appear, and He shall take the church out. That will be the signal that the sun will be coming up pretty soon. However, the Sun is none other that the Sun of Righteousness, the Lord Jesus Christ.

We leave now the Old Testament, where the hope is the coming of Christ to the earth to establish His Kingdom. But in the New Testament we ought to be like the wise men who were looking for the star. We are still to be looking for the Day Star to appear when He will take His church out of this world.

BIBLIOGRAPHY

(Recommended for Further Study)

Feinberg, Charles L. *The Minor Prophets*. Chicago, Illinois: Moody Press, 1976.

Gaebelein, Arno C. *The Annotated Bible*. 1917. Reprint. Neptune, New Jersey: Loizeaux Brothers, 1971.

Ironside, H. A. *The Minor Prophets*. Neptune, New Jersey: Loizeaux Brothers, n.d.

Jensen, Irving L. *Minor Prophets of Judah*. Chicago, Illinois: Moody Press, 1975. (Obadiah, Joel, Micah, Nahum, Zephaniah, and Habakkuk.)

Tatford, Frederick A. *The Minor Prophets*. Minneapolis, Minnesota: Klock & Klock, n.d.

Unger, Merrill F. *Unger's Commentary on the Old Testament*, Vol. 2. Chicago, Illinois: Moody Press, 1982.